Victoria

The *Heart* of *England*

Victoria

The *Heart* of *England*

A JOURNEY OF DISCOVERY

TEXT BY CATHERINE CALVERT

FOREWORD BY SUSAN ALLEN TOTH

AFTERWORD BY NANCY LINDEMEYER

HEARST BOOKS
NEW YORK

It is the policy of William Morrow and Company, Inc., and its imprints and affiliates, recognizing the importance of preserving what has been written, to print the books we publish on acid-free paper, and we exert our best efforts to that end.

Library of Congress Cataloging-in-Publication Data
Victoria, the heart of England : a journey of discovery.
    p. cm.
   Includes index.
   ISBN 0-688-15931-1
   I. England—Civilization.
   DA110.V46   1999
   942—ddc21   98-38491
                                 CIP

Printed in Singapore
This book is set in Centaur.

First Edition

10 9 8 7 6 5 4 3 2 1

For *Victoria* Magazine:

Nancy Lindemeyer—*Editor in Chief*

Susan Maher—*Art Director*

John Mack Carter—*President, Hearst Magazine Enterprises*

www.williammorrow.com

Produced by Smallwood & Stewart, Inc., New York City

Edited by Camilla Crichton

Designed by Debra Sfetsios

Table of Contents

FOREWORD

When I daydream, I often find myself in England. Sometimes I'm hiking along a coastal path in Cornwall, edging my way along the top of a primrose-dotted cliff that plunges down to a restless green sea. As I listen to the surf splashing far below, a cool, damp breeze whiffles through my hair. Sometimes I'm sitting quietly on a rocky tor, looking over rusty bracken tangled with purple heather, under a misty sky that seems to soak into the moor. As far as I can see, treeless hills dip and disappear into the distance. Perhaps I'll hear the high quick trill of a bird or the soft splash of a fast-running stream. But mostly I notice only a deep, satisfying silence.

I daydream about London, too. I'm sitting with a contented sigh in the front seat atop a bright-red double-decker bus, sunning myself on a bench in St. James's Park, strolling with my husband under starlight along the Thames. On a chilly fall day, I can imagine sipping a steaming cup of Earl Grey at Fortnum & Mason, where it always tastes better than tea in my own kitchen.

Of course, my England is highly selective. When I travel there, I seek out charming villages and medieval churches rather than industrial cities and mass housing. A complex and varied country, England today extends far beyond the boundaries of my daydreams. But I do not go to England as a sociologist. I return there again and again because so much nurtures my spirit: its landscape, its architecture and monuments, its literary past, and more—in fact, many of the pleasures and fascinations that lie in the seductive pages of this book. When I can't be in England, I want to read about it.

Susan Allen Toth

The garden at Mottisfont in Hampshire

The lily pond at Tintinhull House

INTRODUCTION

"You that love England, who have an ear for her music . . . " — Cecil Day Lewis

For many of us, the symphony that is England grabs hold of our heart in a single moment. Perhaps it was the day we stepped off the plane and smelled the air, with its redolent scent of green, growing things. Or that first early morning drive: cresting a hill and swooping quietly down on a tiny village still tucked up for the night, roses and hollyhocks tangled all around the cottage doors and windows. Perhaps it was a winter's evening in London, fresh from the theater, when a walk home along the Thames brought a thousand years of history alive in the twinkling towers across the way. Maybe it was the trip around an old house, stuffed with strange collections and glorious art, where the

stories were as good as the furniture. Or perhaps the captivating beat that made our heart skip came from nothing more than a tea cup and saucer tinkling on the train, as the mellow and ancient hills slipped by.

Once we're ensnared by England, it's a love affair that's almost impossible to shake. Whether it's the worldly ways of bustling London that catch the visitor unawares, or the peace and plenty of the countryside, or simply a taste for the novels of Jane Austen and a predilection for tea, this is a country where even armchair travelers can find enjoyment.

Certainly the language is part of the allure, and not just the ease of communication that sharing most of the same speech brings. For those who love words, words whose cadences have been formed by exposure to Shakespeare and Milton, Browning and Brontë, hearing daily the delights of English well spoken, and the modulations of accent and circumstance, is a fascinating journey on its own. Sometimes it is the differences in words that enchant—*lift* and *bonnet* are easy, but do you know *chuffed*? And *fossicking*? Other times, the glory of the language itself mesmerizes. This country talks a lot and talks well—its best newspapers, for instance, are written by columnists who gather up the language and throw it into the air like prestidigitators. And so much of English wit lurks in that same spirit of play, of taking nothing as a certainty. Lewis Carroll and Edward Lear could jumble the words all together and make magic, while P. G. Wodehouse and Austen effortlessly cast down their clever remarks.

Literary references provide a rich backdrop for the traveler. Those characters we've loved and writers we've memorized, whether great or small, bring an evocative aspect to our journey. Is it possible to walk in London without remembering A. A. Milne's—"Bears! I'm walking on squares?" Or to pass Buckingham Palace without thinking of Alice?

Bath and Hampshire come alive for those who love Austen, and so many people travel to the parsonage in Haworth in pursuit of the Brontës that one must go to the moors to find their silences. Beatrix Potter, when seen against the drama of the Lakes, becomes someone else entirely—a student of nature as well as a charming spinner of tales.

London is a myriad of images unto itself. It is Dickens's swirling city with a thousand stories to tell. It belongs to the diarist Pepys, who brings to life old London town. So, too, is it an artist's London: Leighton's Kensington and Hogarth's Chiswick, Turner's Thames. In its familiarity, we feel when we visit as if we are retracing steps we've taken before.

Americans share a history with the English, and exploring theirs serves to illuminate our own. These days, though the cult of modernity is strong in England, the access to the past has never been easier. Museums hum with visitors, and there isn't a corner of the country that does not have a few historic houses open to view, beautifully presented whether publicly or privately owned. Humble cottages dot the landscape as well, along with mills and factories, ships and farmsteads, where time stands still. Everywhere there are churches; step inside, and you're in Norman remains, a medieval masterpiece, or admiring Wren's graceful symmetry or the high-flown sensibilities of Gothic-revival Victorians.

We seek England's history, and perhaps a bit of glamour, in the pageantry that's still a matter of everyday life. Though much of tradition is being stripped away, flapping flags and uniforms, parades and fêtes still touch daily life with magic. Early on a London morning, you might easily be wakened by hoofbeats, and peer out the window to find a regiment of the Household Cavalry going by, spurs jingling. Even as the royal family's doings, once chronicled in glacial nineteenth-century prose in *The Times'* Court Circular, become the stuff of soap opera, the human urge never fades to see the glitter and the glory, to visit Kensington Palace and Windsor Castle, or to find the kings and queens of history entombed in Westminster Abbey.

Oxford city roofscape, the rotunda of the Radcliffe Camera at left

Perhaps the real reason we love England so much is the simple beauty of the place—the roll of the land to the sea, the plunging cliffs, the villages that hide in the lanes, the towns where Georgian crescents and Victorian railway workers' cottages jog along side by side. There's something for every taste. Anyone who loves urban life is smitten by London, where green garden squares are surrounded by tall stately townhouses, and no corner is too mean for a pot of flowers or a flowering vine. The River Thames, a silver ribbon, adds sweep to the city. Though the demise of the village is constantly predicted, there they sit, thatched roofs sheltering householders as they have for centuries, church bells sounding for evensong.

The countryside is a green and pleasant land, truly, where the arrangement of gentle hills and grazing sheep, hedgerows and primroses, ancient barns and prehistoric stones come together in harmony. Travel a bit farther and reach dramatic vistas, where mountain peaks soar, lakes are pale disks beneath a gray sky, and rainstorms whip all to a fury. Carry on and you reach the seaside, with its weather-beaten towns and boardwalks, and the eternal growl of the sea as it dashes itself against the rocks, the white cliffs rising high above the foam.

All in all, this island—poet's prize, nature's beauty—is time's triumph. Come journey with us to explore, and to celebrate, the land we love so well.

Catherine Calvert

TRADITION

The patterns of English life play across the year. Every season has its

certitude—lingering over Sunday lunch in winter, with Yorkshire pud-

dings steaming on a plate; golden summer afternoons, when punters pole

their way on sun-dappled waters. Tradition gilds each moment, as time

slides by in its silent stream.

Tintinhull House in Somerset

To the Manor Born

IF THERE IS AN ART AT WHICH THE ENGLISH EXCEL, SURELY IT IS THE ART of the home—a glorious celebration of domesticity which, over the centuries, has resulted in architecture that invites and interiors that welcome. In country houses such as actress Jane Seymour's home, St. Catherine's Court near Bath, the elements that make a house a home are preserved for each generation to enjoy—the mullioned windows that open to fragrant blossoms, the paths that lead into the well-tended garden, the fireplaces where coals glow, the chimney pots that top the peaked roof where doves coo.

These are charms that reside in houses where countless lives have been sheltered over time. The walls could speak of vanished families—of weddings that filled the halls

The house and garden at St. Catherine's Court near Bath

'Tis very sweet to look into the fair And open face of heaven.

JOHN KEATS

with laughter, of tears that accompanied sons and brothers off to war, of toasting crumpets in the nursery fireplace, of a rose bush blooming for its hundredth spring. This is bedrock beauty, the sort that lasts forever. For a nation that sent so many across the sea, surely it was the thought of these home fires burning that warmed their journeys.

In English country houses, perfection is never the goal. It is comfort that lies at the heart of English domesticity and country-house style.

A sitting room, for example, is

The drawing room at St. Catherine's Court

The sitting room in the London home of ceramic designer Emma Bridgewater, opposite, and a detail, above

always a patchwork of a family's tastes, history, hobbies, and time together. An ancient Scrabble board is wedged into the bookcase, and the bits unbroken from Great-Granny's tea service now march across the mantel. There might be faded watercolors of the sea, oil paintings of beloved views, an aging mirror in a magnificent (but now sadly chipped and timeworn) gilt frame, a toppling stack of books, a rug that belongs to the dog. Usually there is something bizarre, always the source of much hilarity—an umbrella stand shaped like a guardsman, perhaps, foolishly brought home by Grandfather as a souvenir of his time in Madras—and always useful for breaking the ice with first-time guests.

But the important things are always right: the bellows beside the fireplace, the well-stocked drinks cupboard, the pillows piled high, the tables that can be pulled into place for the tea tray or an after-dinner card game, the flowers brought in from the garden and thrust haphazardly into a vase. Individual, yet unremarkable,

An Englishwoman's Retreat

Today's England preserves many of the traditions that once divided life into woman's world, man's world: Old boys still gather in gentlemen's clubs to reminisce about schoolboy pranks, and invitations are still given and received in the name of the lady of the house. And if a man's club is in London's St. James's, hung with portraits of presidents past and full of squashy leather chairs, a woman might well hold out for a quiet corner of the house to make her own. When Virginia Woolf called for

"a room of one's own," she was speaking of its importance to the creative woman, but every woman knows the joy to be found in a place for quiet contemplation.

A hundred years ago it would have been her bedroom, where she breakfasted off a tray, opened the mail, wrote some notes; or the morning room, where she instructed the housekeeper and entertained her callers. But today's Englishwoman, lacking staff and leisure time, must create where she can—a corner of the sitting room, a well-organized desk in the kitchen, a soft chair pulled up by the fire in the drawing room, a well-stocked gardener's bench.

these are rooms that invite you to sit and stay awhile.

Perhaps the English gift for cozy domesticity is simply a matter of coping with an unpredictable climate; when the wind is apt to turn and the rain to beat against the windowpanes, shelter and warmth take on an added importance. Happy is the woman who knows that when she gets home there will be thick curtains to draw, shutting out the world. There will be a properly made pot of tea and a battered chair begging her to sink into its softness, the two cushions placed just so. Upstairs, brimming with lavish chintz and lace, there

An Englishwoman's bedroom, and a dressing table at Hambleton Hall Hotel in Rutland, left

will be family photographs on her dressing table, some lavender water in a bottle, and a soft mattress and downy comforter. In this little nest are all of life's pleasures, and dreams, too.

This is a litany for life that has evolved from Elizabethan days, when the master and mistress retired to their "withdrawing room" for time alone, away from the hustle and bustle of the household, and they furnished their retreat with creature comforts.

Since then English homes have developed so that a house might bear

WRAPPING A ROOM IN WARMTH

The English enthusiasm for curtains is, like so many things, the result of making a virtue out of necessity. Living in centuries-old houses where there are only so many seats by the fire, and where the wind whistles through Georgian sashes or Victorian plate-glass windows, comfort and warmth are always a priority. Until two hundred years ago, internal shutters sufficed for most, though the very wealthy might have hung a tapestry over a window. Then the Georgians, with their exquisite taste and sense of proportion, began to hang cloth at their larger paned windows—always in measured amounts, however, as printed cloth was expensive. When the mills of the Victorian age began to produce comparatively cheap bales of fabric, the taste for drapery grew: The magic of drawing curtains to stem the approaching darkness and winter chill proved irresistible. Styles and fashions developed fast, so that the swags and tails, festoons, and pelmets that mark today's decorating trends have as much to do with tradition as they do with keeping warm. Sketches by the eighteenth-century designer Thomas Chippendale included designs for drawn-up tops, and they have remained a favorite window treatment ever since (right).

Tradition 27

The summer house at St. Catherine's Court

traces of every era: the Georgian sense of proportion and space, the Victorian passion for pattern and comfort and amusing objects to please the eye, the Edwardian love of the rituals of the dining table and the bath.

These remnants linger because they belong to a shared family past—it's not unusual in England to discover that one house has been inhabited by the same family for generations—and because of an ingrained thrifty sense—that a well-placed darn or glue on a broken plate will do (besides, it was one of Grand-mother's wedding gifts and it is not worn-out quite yet, just a bit careworn).

This reverence for tradition and need for comfort and shelter are evident in every corner of the house and even spill out into the garden, just in case the weather should be kind. Doors open onto a terrace where honeysuckle wafts its heavenly scent, a summer-house is equipped with inviting cushions, a table is set up for lunch under a cherry tree, blossoms falling all around.

Who could question that these are houses full of charm and tranquility, with rooms that speak directly to every compassionate heart?

THE GENTLEWOMAN'S SPORT OF CHOICE

"Chess on grass" is how the best players refer to croquet. Those who think of croquet as no more than an amusing way to while away an afternoon, or as a game that only children can enjoy, haven't played croquet in an English country garden. For in England, croquet is a very civilized form of combat—and war it is. The beautifully manicured croquet lawn becomes a battlefield, and only cunning strategy and a little skill can secure a win, with balls placed just so to block an opponent, and a lot of quiet but oh-so-fervid rejoicing when, with a loud smack of mallet to ball, the careful planning is revealed.

The Victorians loved the game, not least because it was an acceptable way for young men and women to get together while chaperones dozed in wicker chairs under a shady tree. Besides, without any lack of decorum a young lady could show a fetching display of ankle every time she bent to her ball.

Today, an area of the English garden is still often set aside for the game, with carefully groomed grass to ensure the balls roll straight and true. Croquet sets, beautifully crafted and packed in their own leather cases or polished wooden trunks, are a proud feature of the tangle of sports equipment in the hall of every country house. And, as ever, the quiet languor of a summer Sunday afternoon is interrupted by the triumphant cheers of those who've set up wickets on the lawn.

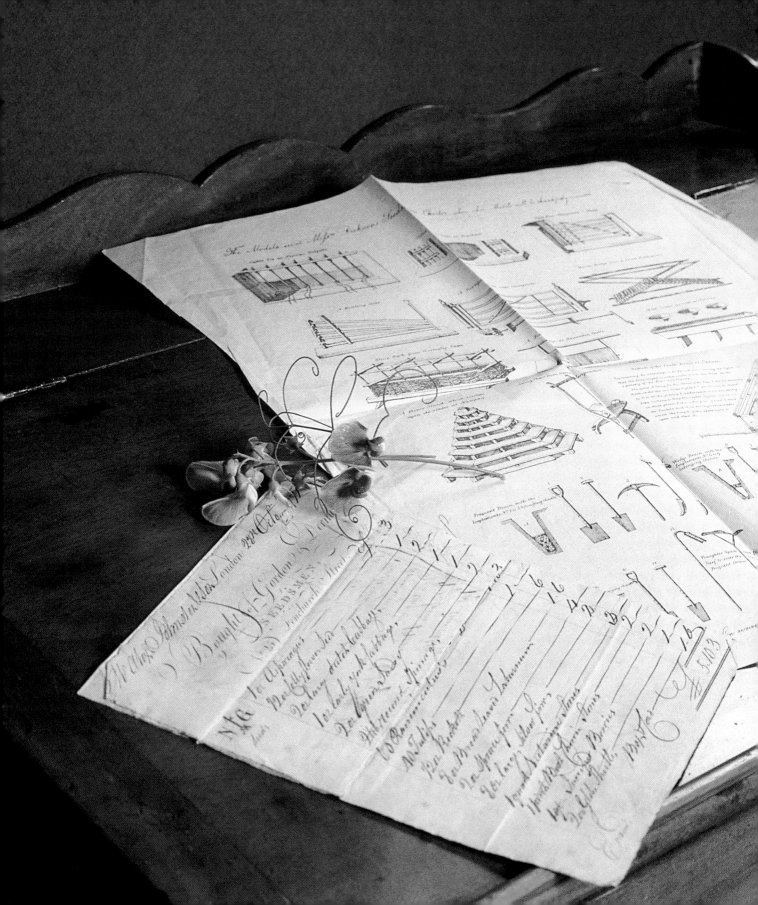

The Glory of England

THERE IS SOMETHING ABOUT THE LIGHT IN ENGLAND THAT BRINGS color to life. Even on a cloudy day, flowers seem to glow despite the gloom, while on a sun-struck afternoon, a kaleidoscope of color whirls around you. And sometimes it seems as though all the world's in bloom, and England another Eden. There's no end to the paradise—when dooryards fill with lilac blossoms, when bluebells carpet a woodland floor, when daffodils outline the curve of a hill, when even schoolyards are high with hollyhocks. Wherever you look, the earth leaps into color, and reigning over all the beauty are England's gardens, her crowning glory.

So it is only right and proper that the country's great gardeners should be held in the

Gertrude Jekyll's gardening lists, opposite, and the maze at Hatfield House in Hertfordshire

Where're you tread, the blushing flow'rs shall rise, And all things flourish where you turn your eyes.

ALEXANDER POPE

An exhibit at The Museum of Garden History in London

The designs of Gertrude Jekyll are preserved like fine antiques, for these are the gardens where the now-venerated skill of building a border was originated. In particular there is her pride and joy—Munstead Wood, in Surrey, recently restored.

Jekyll, who began the garden in 1888, lavished fifty years of planning and care to create, with her painter's eye, luscious borders dense with color, and plantings that change with the seasons. Elements that would be debits in the hands of less gifted gardeners—shade and damp, dense thickets of trees—were turned to advantage. Each spring, primroses spread like sparkling yellow stars in the shadows of the trees. There is the heath garden, the rock garden, the fern walks, and the paths lined with blooming beauties—azaleas in their full maturity. By selecting plants and shrubs that would thrive in this fifteen-acre landscape of towering trees, Jekyll successfully united the old and new traditions of formal and informal garden design, establishing a standard that other gardeners strive for to this day.

highest esteem. Names like John Tradescant, Lancelot "Capability" Brown, Vita Sackville-West, and Gertrude Jekyll inspire instantaneous respect, even reverence, and they speak to us still through the plants and gardens they left behind.

Pilgrims throng to Vita Sackville-West's Sissinghurst garden in Kent, especially treasuring her groundbreaking all-white garden "room." The legacy of the great "Capability" Brown is everywhere evident in the careful designs of the estate gardens that surround many of England's grandest country houses and mansions.

The main border at Munstead Wood in Surrey

Modern-day gardeners are helping to keep alive the heritage of their renowned predecessors. Rosemary Verey, Penelope Hobhouse, and Rosemary Nicholson, for example, whose books are blueprints for gardeners everywhere, combine the best of the past with their own emotional perspective and artistic interpretation.

On behalf of The National Trust, Penelope Hobhouse brought a fresh eye to the color wheel of heritage gardening at Tintinhull House in Somerset, where she created a magnificent garden using traditional elements such as lily ponds and box-lined paths.

But perhaps it is to Rosemary Nicholson that we owe the biggest debt. The story begins some fifteen years ago, when she visited the site of the derelict church of St. Mary-at-Lambeth in

A POTTER AT WORK IN THE GARDEN

The humble terra-cotta pot must be one of mankind's most ancient accomplishments, and they are as basic to the well-tended English garden as roses and latticework. Containers full of plants have long been used to decorate all those spots—on the terrace, down the front steps—where earth and flower beds don't quite reach, and for nurturing young and tender plants in the greenhouse and kitchen garden. Terra-cotta is perfect because it is porous and can breathe, giving roots the air they need; Water also evaporates through the pot's sides, keeping roots cool in summer, while the thickness keeps them safe in winter.

Some of the handsomest pots in England are made by Jim Keeling, a former archeology student who's traded hunting for potsherds with his trowel for throwing pots on a wheel. He's also brought new life to his small village in the Cotswolds with

the cottage industry he calls Whichford Pottery. Every piece is carefully handmade by Keeling or a local employee, whether spun on a wheel or pressed into a mold. The resulting pots are then decorated with swags, lions' heads, or even a family crest for a unique and personal variation on this common English form.

So successful has he been that Keeling now produces more than a hundred pot gardens for the Chelsea Flower Show each year. Not surprisingly, gardening in terra-cotta is also one of Keeling's passions. "Making good pots, beautiful pots, is not unlike gardening," he says. "You're working with the stuff of the earth, and it's a process you have to guide carefully all the way."

The knot garden at The Museum of Garden History

search of the grave of John Tradescant, the brilliant gardener to Charles I. Tradescant spent much of his life traveling the globe in search of new shrubs and flowers, bringing them home to glorify the king's gardens.

Upon finding his grave, Nicholson was inspired to organize a trust to rescue the church in which he was buried and to reopen it as a museum to celebrate England's garden heritage.

Today, The Museum of Garden History lies tucked away from traffic's roar on the south bank of the Thames in London. The former church contains a delightful jumble of special exhibitions and a small collection on permanent display: Gertrude Jekyll's desk, gardening lists, and sketches, for example, and fine old garden tools.

Meanwhile, rising from the once-overgrown churchyard is a new garden planted to old designs. It features a knot garden with box borders and plants that would have been well known to seventeenth-century English gardeners like Tradescant but are rarely found today.

Preserving the Past

EACH DAY IN ENGLAND FINDS THE PAST PRESSING CLOSE TO THE present. Footsteps tread where ancients have gone before, down paths thousands of years old; church bells ring in the same patterns they've always followed; houses sit in gardens tenderly planted centuries ago; and portraits of ancestors gaze down from gilded frames upon descendants, the family likeness there for everyone to see. Though often considered the most modern of European nations, England has a taproot of tradition that links yesterday to today in ways that enrich each and every moment. Preserving the past is as instinctive to the English as making tea at four o'clock.

But there have been times this century when the riches and rituals of the past have been

Recipe books at Petworth House in West Sussex, opposite, and the Syon House dining room in Middlesex

A thing of beauty is a joy forever. It's loveliness increases; it will never pass into nothingness . . .

JOHN KEATS

cottages, as well as woods and forests, farms and fields, mountain ranges, and stretches of the seashore—the very substance of the country.

On occasion owners turned over a house with its contents intact—and then what delights there were to be discovered. Perhaps some beautifully illustrated, handwritten Georgian recipe books might be found on a dusty shelf in a long-forgotten pantry. Or a debutante's ball gowns may have been carefully packed away in a trunk at the end of the season a century ago, only to be unpacked decades later. Mr. Straw's House, a modest Edwardian workingman's cottage in Nottinghamshire, was discovered with its interior frozen in time, every detail from the 1930s undisturbed, down to the washcloths beside the basin and the newspaper on the parlor table.

To bring these places back to life, old skills have had to be revived and long-lost techniques brought to bear. The furniture in houses under The National Trust's auspices are dusted with feathers and polished with beeswax and soft cloths. With

overlooked. Between the two World Wars, for example, many of the great houses were left abandoned: empty and echoing, inhabited only by ghosts. Few people had the wherewithal to lay a glittering table, like that at Syon House (previous page), which is set just as it would have been for a visit by the young Princess Victoria in the 1820s.

In the latter part of the twentieth century, it has been the job of organizations such as The National Trust and English Heritage to preserve the treasures of the past. Wherever there was history and an uncertain future, these groups have stepped in to rescue ancient castles, grand mansions and palaces, manor houses, and humble

Polishing copper pots at Lanhydrock House in Cornwall, opposite, and accoutrements of Victorian cooking on the kitchen table at Petworth House

When sixteenth-century English traders returned home from China, they carried

exquisite treasure in their holds—porcelain unique in its quality and design. Before

long, the demand for this elegant new tableware was such that enterprising manu-

facturers began to experiment with ways to imitate it.

By the end of the eighteenth century, the taste for china was no longer depen-

dent on the far-away kilns of the Orient, and Staffordshire had become the center

of a thriving industry, manufacturing all that was required to gracefully set a table.

Two of the best and most successful designers were Thomas Minton and Josiah

Spode, whose factories still produce beautiful china tea sets and dinner services.

Queen Victoria so loved Minton's designs that she called them "the most beau-

tiful in the world." Admirers of

Spode come to marvel at the Blue

Room in the Spode Museum, with its antique examples of classic transferware

designs (a process of transferring intricate engravings from copperplate to dinner

plate, perfected by Josiah Spode). There are now over 25,000 Spode patterns.

But close to the heart of many is the world-famous blue and white landscape that

dates back to 1790, and which Spode still produces—the bridge and tree pattern,

modeled after the Chinese original, and known as the Blue Willow pattern.

painstaking care and elbow grease, an age-old recipe is used to bring to a glow the copper pots found in the Victorian kitchens at Lanhydrock in Cornwall.

To achieve historical accuracy, scholars such as Peter Brears and artists such as Margaret Murton are brought in. Brears enjoys nothing more than foraging through old recipe books to find out just what the cook would have served at a dinner party in 1899, and Murton spends hours recreating historic tapestry designs for The National Trust's textiles department.

In preserving England's heritage so scrupulously, these experts give an incomparable gift, which lies in the memories taken away by visitors: the way the sun falls on the well-rubbed mahogany of an armchair, the garden path that leads through a maze of ancient box, with a scent like no other.

And now the halls and stairways, kitchens and bedrooms of these reburnished treasures draw those who love beauty and who seek history, and echo to living voices once more.

The tools of Margaret Murton's tapestry work

RECRAFTING THE PAST FOR FILM

The English fascination with their past is nowhere better illustrated than in the films and television series we've enjoyed over the years, where every detail of period life is correct, right down the the buttons on a waistcoat and the clock on a mantel. It was the television classic *Upstairs, Downstairs* that set the standard, but lavish productions such as *A Room with a View, Howard's End*, and *Sense and Sensibility* have recreated the past with a thrilling, exquisite conviction.

Precise detail and historical accuracy are the result of a lot of expert research. Film producers hire the best in the business to provide props for their sets and cos-

tumes for their actors—prop houses like Farley's and costumers such as Jenny Bevan and John Bright at CosProp.

Farley's has an enormous collection of household paraphernalia from every era—inkstands, candlesticks, goblets, picture frames, carpets, and so on—everything, in fact, that a

filmmaker might need to reassemble a seventeenth-century ballroom or Victorian drawing room.

Similarly, CosProp boasts an enormous collection of clothes and accoutrements—parasols, capes, spats, lace caps, petticoats and stays, and more—that span the centuries and are suitable for any occasion, from an Edwardian tennis match to a stroll through the eighteenth-century streets of London. When the actors arrive on set and don their costumes, even the undergarments are perfect. With such proper attire, an actor's interpretation can spring to life, and a viewer be happily enchanted.

Making Merry at Christmas

CHRISTMAS IN ENGLAND HAS LONG BEEN A TIME OF REVELS AND RITUALS. In the Middle Ages, the celebrations fell under the realm of the Lord of Misrule, a member of the royal court who was appointed to supervise the festivities; as his name suggests, Christmas was a period of licensed disorder.

In the mid-nineteenth century, Prince Albert introduced a number of embellishments to Christmas at Queen Victoria's court, and it is in Victorian times that the origins of much of today's Christmas lie—in the candlelit tree, presents underneath, the emphasis on children—because what the court did, the country copied, as had always been the way. Soon the festival incorporated much more of what the Victorians loved—the meals with many courses, the

Decorated for Christmas, the Lucknam Park Hotel in Wiltshire

I will honor Christmas in my heart, and try to keep it all the year.

CHARLES DICKENS

opportunity to dress up, the chance to send the new greeting cards (first offered in 1849). With Charles Dickens as chronicler, the Victorian family Christmas became the ideal, from stuffed turkey to "God bless us every one."

In England everyone heads home for the holiday—whether that's a London townhouse, a cottage in the Lake District, or a Cotswold mansion—and there the family gathers, perhaps for the first time since the previous Christmas.

But the holiday excitement really begins with the drama of anticipation, and the preparation that's all part and parcel of the season. In England, this means shopping under the bright and festive lights of London's Regent Street, or heading off to towns like Bath.

Then there will be outings and treats for the children, especially the eagerly anticipated visit to Santa in his tinsel-wrapped "grotto," surrounded by his elves.

Afterward it's home again, arms laden, to settle down with a cup of tea and paper and scissors, ribbons and bows, to carefully wrap up gifts for everyone. Or perhaps to write some more Christmas cards, and later to open the ones that arrived in the mail that morning and march them across the mantel. And still the tree needs trimming, with ornaments that have graced the family's trees for generations. With so much to do, thank heavens the menu remains the same.

The country comes to a stop on Christmas Eve, when the roads fill with travelers anxious to get home. The evening is full of quiet revelry, until it's time to go to church, sing carols, and listen as the joyous bells ring out their midnight message.

Then the long-awaited Christmas morning arrives. Oh, the wonder of waking up to find a lumpy stocking hanging on the bedpost. Although full of surprises, the stocking contains one certainty: There will be a tangerine in the toe. Everyone has a stocking—this is a gift for the child in everyone.

By lunchtime, the house is full of fragrances: of baking pies and roasting turkey or pheasant, of sausages sizzling, and of pudding steaming. The

The tree and grandfather clock at Michael's Nook Country House Hotel in Grasmere, in the spirit of the season

table is beautifully laid with the best china, silver, and crystal, and, most importantly, Christmas crackers—the brightly wrapped tubes filled with treats—one at every place and more piled in the center.

As soon as everybody is seated, arms link to tug on the cracker ends. And POP! a cascade of bad jokes and tiny toys tumbles out. In barely a minute all have donned their silly paper hats and read the jokes aloud, and the most enterprising of the children has bargained hard and scooped up all the toys.

With great ceremony, the roast is carried in, to unanimous marveling, and with it the chestnuts and the sausages, the bread sauce and the Brussels sprouts. Everyone eats too much but can still manage just one more bite.

The most dramatic moment is still to come: the appearance of the Christmas pudding, topped with holly and flaming in brandy. Brandy butter and small mince pies fill the plates until it's only possible to eat the bitter chocolate mint that arrives with the coffee at the end of the meal.

Afternoons are for snoozing, or for a brisk walk before the early darkness. ("Let's try to work off lunch.") Everybody must be back in time to listen, with respect, to the Queen's Speech, which is broadcast over the radio and on the television.

Then it's time for tea, and another sliver of the Christmas cake, until, at last, it's present-opening time (the children have been so patient). Somebody, perhaps Uncle, dresses up in the old Father Christmas suit and distributes the gifts all around.

Tomorrow will be Boxing Day, traditionally the day when boxes of food are given to the poor; it is also a day for reflection and for the renewal of old friendships. But that is still to come. Tonight, everyone finds a comfortable spot and settles in for an evening around the fire, telling stories, laughing, and enjoying being together, until someone foolishly suggests a game of charades and the party dissolves into giggles.

This is a heartwarming Christmas, in all its holly-wreathed, red-bowed, and candlelit beauty.

Poet of the Lakes

"WHAT HAPPY FORTUNE WERE IT HERE TO LIVE!" WROTE WILLIAM Wordsworth, the poet whose love of the English countryside brought his art to its finest flowering. As he paced the paths and tramped the hills of his beloved Lake District—where the clouds' gray billows are caught on the waves of the water, and daffodils pour a stream of gold down the hillside each spring—he composed his verse in his head, capturing the very spirit of his age. Inspired by the beauty he saw around him, Wordsworth wrought art from nature, finding eternity in the shift of the seasons.

Born in the Lake District in 1770, the young William was raised in a succession of small towns after the death of his parents. But he cherished his early childhood memories of

In the Lake District, daffodils bloom, opposite, and hills rise over the water

'Tis the sense of majesty, and beauty, and repose, A blended holiness of earth and sky . . .

WILLIAM WORDSWORTH

freedom in the hills—

Fair seed-time had my soul, and I grew up
Fostered alike by beauty and by fear;
Much favored in my birthplace

—so that when he commenced the poetry-making that was his life's work, he was drawn to return to the land that had once spread its beauty around him.

In 1799, he brought his sister, Dorothy, with him to settle at Dove Cottage in the small town of Grasmere. The two had a warm and sympathetic relationship: Dorothy had always been his devoted confidante, and he relied upon her greatly for encouragement.

Together they swept and tidied the little cottage, hung curtains at the windows, and began the first of the gardens that would always bring joy to their lives.

Wordsworth was drawn outside every day, even when the clouds boiled with rain over the lakes. He knew there would be the warmth of the fireside, and his sister's friendship and note-taking (her own *Grasmere Journal* provides a fascinating insight into their lives together), to return to.

So he tramped the hills, walking as many as thirty miles a day, chanting his verses aloud as he went. "Nine-tenths of my verses have been murmured out in the open air," he later wrote. He found his themes and his philosophy—the discovery of God's hand all around him—in the harmony and fierce beauty of nature. He stated it clearly, as he felt—

A presence that disturbs me with the joy
Of elevated thoughts; a sense sublime
Of something far more deeply interfused,
Whose dwelling is the light of setting suns
And the round ocean and the living air
And the blue sky, and in the mind of man.

Wordsworth's solitude vanished when other poets, and fame, eventually found him. He became the center of a circle that included Robert Southey and Samuel Taylor Coleridge. Together the three poets became known as the Lake Poets, and the time they spent in Grasmere was chronicled in poetry, diaries, and letters, in a fertile cross-pollination of creativity and intellect.

As his fame grew, Wordsworth moved to nearby Rydal Mount. There he lived for the rest of his life, in a gracious house surrounded by gardens he planted as carefully as he crafted his poetry, and with the same intent—"to assist Nature in moving the affections." These were years of contentment and success. In 1843, he succeeded his old friend Southey as Poet Laureate, which required his presence at the Royal Court from time to time.

Images from Wordsworth's life: his satchel, opposite top; first home, Dove Cottage at Grasmere, opposite bottom; and Rydal Mount at Ambleside, above, where he spent his final years

But he was sustained by life's quieter pleasures: the hills and lakes, his beloved garden—

O happy Garden! whose seclusion deep
Hath been so friendly to industrious hours;
And to soft slumbers, that did gently steep
Our spirits, carrying with them dreams
of flowers,
And wild notes warbled among leafy bowers.

Today, the many visitors who venture to Wordsworth's land of lakes can still hear his voice—it's there in the "host of golden daffodils" blooming at the water's edge, upon which he "gazed—and gazed—but little thought/ What wealth the show to me had brought," singing of the secrets he shares with those who hear poetry in the breeze.

. . . *Who could look*

And not feel motions there? I thought of clouds

That sail on winds; of breezes that delight

To play on water, or in endless chase

Pursue each other through the liquid depths

Of grass of corn, over and through and through,

In billow after billow evermore;

Of sunbeams, shadows, butterflies, and birds,

Angels and winged creatures that are lords

Without restraint of all which they behold.

I sat, and stirred in spirit as I looked,

I seemed to feel such liberty was mine,

Such power and joy; but only for this end:

To flit from field to rock, from rock to field,

From shore to island, and from isle to shore,

From open place to covert, from a bed

Of meadow-flowers into a tuft of wood,

From high to low, from low to high, yet still

Within the bounds of this huge concave; here

Should be my home, this valley be my world.

William Wordsworth
Home at Grasmere

WIT AND CHARM

It's a great English tradition that nothing should be taken too seriously. Light-

heartedness is the kind of grace that makes the difficult look easy, the mundane

more sparkling—why not hang one's gardening hat over a statue in the hall?

And in a country that so loves words, wit is the playing field where wordsmiths

romp and nothing's too sacred for a joke.

A scene from Rosemary Verey's garden

The Rites of Spring

AN ENGLISH SPRING IS A SUBTLE THING, A WATERCOLOR BEAUTY THAT steals upon you unawares, as the trees gradually turn green, the daffodils unfurl, and the first brave roses bud and reach. Some days the rain pours down, a chill wind blows, and everyone huddles and scuttles for home, lays the fire yet one more time, and pulls a chair up close. Then morning arrives, and the air is lively with scent and sound, the garden fragrant with blossoms, the breeze gentle on the skin. Spring has slipped in once again.

After the long dark winter, the arrival of spring is marked by joyful celebration—as it has been since the beginning of time—and age-old ways are reawakened. On the first day of May each year, villagers gather so that nimble hands can fashion garlands, wreaths, and a

The May Queen. opposite, and two of her attendants

*'Tis a month before the month of May,
And the Spring comes slowly up this way . . .*

SAMUEL TAYLOR COLERIDGE

bower for the May Queen, a young girl chosen from the village. The Maypole, freshly painted, is dressed with ribbons and erected on the green. Tables are set up nearby, in a shady spot under the newly blossoming trees in the orchard, for there will be feasting later. Morris dancers shake out their bells and ribbons to practice steps and measures that date from the fifteenth century.

The Morris Dance is heavy with drums, the beat of sticks, the jingle of bells, and has an earthy, fundamental rhythm. It holds a symbolic and important place in the May Day pageant. The dance recounts legends,

On May Day, Morris dancers tread their measures, and apple trees flower

in particular the story of Robin Hood and his Merry Men: Each of the dancers adopts a character for the performance and the May Queen appears as Maid Marian.

Afterward the children, giggling with excitement and delight, gather round the Maypole, treading on each others' toes. As they skip and sing, ribbon in hand, twisting in and out, the beauty slowly grows. The May Queen looks on, reigning over all for the day. Crowned with flowers, she sits in her bower, radiant and blossoming like the cherry trees. In the words of Alfred, Lord Tennyson in his poem *The May Queen*—

You must wake and call me early, call me
*   early, mother dear;*
Tomorrow 'ill be the happiest time of all the
*   glad New Year;*
Of all the glad New Year, mother, the
*   maddest, merriest day;*
For I'm to be Queen o' the May, mother,
*   I'm to be Queen o' the May.*

In marking the end of winter and the commencement of the planting and growing season, May Day is all about hopes and wishes for the future: the success of the coming harvest, the unity of family and community, the lasting happiness of the small ones who tumble, chuckling, in the grass.

And as the dancing ends and the feasting begins, a confetti cloud of apple blossoms will surely drift to the earth—Mother Nature's own eternal rite of spring.

Children entwine the Maypole in Devon

Fruit of Common Ground

A DOZEN OR SO COTTAGES, A CHURCH, A RECTORY FOR THE VICAR, A schoolhouse for the children—a village lies snug around its green. And always, in every village, there was the common ground where the community's sheep could graze, sheltered from sun and rain by the spreading boughs of apple trees. Because once upon a time every town, every village, and, in fact, every farm in England had an orchard.

In the past, apples were one of the country's bounties, their varieties endless—6,000 kinds were counted in the last century. Full of juice and succulence, sharp or sweet, made for eating or grown for cooking, they came with thoroughly local names that sound as if they might be poems—Cornish Gilliflowers and Devonshire Quarrendens, for example.

In Northamptonshire, the kitchen at Sulgrave Manor, opposite, and 'May Queen' apples

*In this sequestered nook
how sweet
To sit upon
my orchard-seat!*

WILLIAM WORDSWORTH

Sorting the apples from a bountiful harvest, which might include the 'Cox Orange Pippin,' introduced in 1825, below

But those were the days when farm laborers were paid partly in cider, the drink made from apples that was the beverage of the working classes. Then, at the end of the last century, wage laws were reformed, fewer cider apples were needed, and the orchards were gradually abandoned.

Today, changing farming methods and tastes have reduced the range of apples to half a dozen. Counties that once shimmered with the palest pink blossoms in springtime—Sussex, Dorset, Kent—have lost almost all of their orchards. And that means that apple varieties, some dating back to medieval times, are quietly disappearing, too.

But not altogether, because fortunately there are people like Sue Clifford and Angela King, who, with a concern that village life was rapidly disappearing and a mind for preservation, founded Common Ground to conserve the flavorful local culture of England's parishes and villages.

One of the results of their work, and that of hundreds and thousands of others, is that old orchards are beginning to bloom again, and villagers are coming together to rediscover their apple heritage. Festivals such as the one now held annually at Sulgrave Manor in Oxfordshire celebrate bountiful apple harvests with storytelling, cider-pressing demonstrations, and apple tastings, establishing a tradition that will unite the community for generations to come.

From the seaside hamlets of Devon and Cornwall to the rolling farmland of Wiltshire, ancient orchards that lay untended for years are now laden with fruit. Heirloom varieties, thought to be gone forever, are turning up all over the country: In Purley they rediscovered Brown Snout, while Handsome Norman hangs heavy upon the boughs in Much Marcle. These rediscovered varieties have passionate admirers, each of whom has a favorite for a pie or a sauce, or as a complement to a walk.

The English Eccentric

THE ENGLISH HAVE THE ENDEARING KNACK OF BEING PERFECTLY capable of entertaining two contradictory ideas at the same time; in fact, they make an art of it. So it comes as no surprise that a country that is in many ways fundamentally conservative, with rituals unchanged for hundreds of years, can have room for—even be amused by and positively admire—people who march to their own drum. Indeed, quite often, they march to the tune of their own entire brass band.

This tolerance of eccentrics—those who make living as they please an expression of individuality—is to be found at every level of society and permeates and flavors everyday life: Just look at the hats at Ascot and the straight faces on those sporting them. As long as you

Miniature homes in the Model Village in Bourton-on-the-Water

Always is to joy inclin'd, Lawless, wing'd, and unconfin'd, And breaks all chains from every mind . . .

WILLIAM BLAKE

seem fairly ordinary when compared to one man's collection of barbed wire, or a pop-scholarly assembly of Victorian loos. Clearly, such passions are a direct result of the eighteenth-century interest in science, and the nineteenth-century craze for collecting examples of anything and everything.

Then there are the even more ambitious "grand eccentrics." The National Trust preserves at least three different houses where the inhabitants stopped the clock in 1930 or 1890 or 1780—never installing electricity nor moving a vase put in place generations before—and countless "follies" built

have enough self-confidence (a little imagination helps) you can carry anything off, and set yourself apart from the admiring crowd. Even Sir Winston Churchill, in the midst of winning World War II, found time to design velvet boiler suits so that he could meet his generals in comfort!

A person's hobby is often the best indicator of eccentricity. Surely more people pursue private passions in England than anywhere else. Collectors all over the country avidly seek out the arcane. Thimbles and fans, bird's eggs and butterflies, fossils and buttons: All

over the centuries by wealthy eccentrics. Take the unique sixteen-sided house in Devon, for example. Named A La Ronde, the house was built toward the end of the eighteenth century on the instructions of two spinster cousins after they returned home from a tour of Europe. The house also boasts an extraordinary interior that includes a feather frieze and a room encrusted with seashells.

Latter-day examples of the same kinds of originality abound, such as the astonishing treehouses built by those who love life above ground, or the burrows tunneled by those who prefer life below. Frequently the expression of grand eccentricity results in a marvel, like the miniature village—perfect in every way—that was built as a labor of love in the Cotswolds during the 1930s.

Then there's the gentleman who is building an airplane in his cellar, the fellow who's constructing a submarine in his garage, and the curator who always dresses as a nineteenth-century dandy. Wonderful people, they're all about the place.

Overlooking the Wiltshire countryside, opposite top; life in the trees, opposite bottom and above

Treasure Chest of Toys

JUST AS IN THE REST OF THE WORLD, BEING A CHILD IN THE NOT-SO-long-ago English past wasn't always easy, even for the wealthiest children. The lucky ones grew up with memories of halcyon nursery days. Others, should they make it past babyhood, faced the awfulness of boarding school—with cold showers, rigorous sports, and Latin verbs to contend with—and the era's strict ethos that "children shall be seen but not heard."

But what the children did have were toys, beautiful toys. Many live on, too precious to dispose of, as treasures brought down from the attic on special occasions for the next generation of children to marvel at. London museums, such as The Museum of Childhood in Bethnal Green, are full of wonder: beautifully wrought examples of the toymaker's

A delightful dollhouse shop, opposite, and the nursery at Lanhydrock House in Cornwall

There is always a moment in childhood when the door opens and lets the future in.

GRAHAM GREENE

Favorite English toys include beloved teddy bears from Canterbury Bears, above; a rocking horse, right; and a miniature tea set made for Queen Victoria by Minton, opposite

skillful art. They are fascinating to look at, not only because of their craftsmanship but because they give us a glimpse of what life was like, in miniature, all those years ago.

As Victorian factories hummed with well-made goods for grownups, children's needs were catered to as well: scaled-down stoves made of real iron, with petite pots; tiny tea sets, perfect in every detail, created by the finest china manufacturers to teach young girls the proper techniques of the teatime ritual (some sets even had instructive aphorisms on the plates).

Another favorite for girls were the marvelous dolls, always accompanied by trunks full of pint-sized clothes. One wax-headed baby doll came with flowing lawn dresses, and another, a very grown-up fashion doll, with a selection of ever-so-small pearl-buttoned kid gloves and a choice of ball gowns.

Oh, and the dollhouses—complete to the very last doorknob, from the mouse in the kitchen to the cat curled up on the four-poster bed in the master bedroom. To while away the hours after church on Sunday afternoons, when no properly raised child was allowed to do anything "unimproving," there were Noah's arks, with parades of animals, two by two, carved out of wood.

Children could be taken off to the park with hoops and balls, wagons with iron wheels, and sleds emblazoned with mottos. Little boys played with battalions of toy soldiers, cast in lead and beautifully painted in the uniforms of the latest military campaign.

Animals were never far away: Rocking horses that saw many a mile roll by, real horsehair manes flapping and saddle bells tinkling, were always a favorite, and are still crafted today. So too were cuddly toys, especially teddy bears—a reliable ear for childish

secrets, a snug armful for a quiet moment. Small children off to boarding school were allowed to bring their bears, at least for the first year, and rows of dormitory beds each had a lop-eared, rubbed-to-a-nub Edward, there for a comforting hug at the end of the day.

Inspired by Nature

"I DO NOT REMEMBER A TIME WHEN I DID NOT TRY TO INVENT pictures and make fairy tales—amongst the wild flowers, the animals, trees and mosses and fungi—all the thousand common objects of the countryside, that pleasant unchanging world of realism and romance . . . " wrote Beatrix Potter. The union of fantasy and the natural world makes up much of her appeal: Turn the leaves of *The Tale of Peter Rabbit* and each button, each carrot top is detailed in delicate watercolor and subtle pastel tones.

Potter, the only child of strict Victorian parents, spent her own childhood in the nursery at the top of the house, with a governess and a nanny for company. Despite all those discouraging stairs, the lonely little girl managed to harbor rabbits and field mice, lizards, a

An illustration by Beatrix Potter, opposite, and a view of her Lake District countryside

Childhood, catching our imagination when it is fresh and tender, never lets go of us.

J. B. PRIESTLEY

bat, and a family of snails. They were her passion and treasury as she began to draw, and in capturing their likenesses on paper she developed her exquisitely fine sense of observation as well as her remarkable skills with pen and brush.

When she was old enough to leave her parents' home, Potter moved to a Lake District farm, in Sawrey, where she raised sheep and eventually married a farmer. The natural world continued to inspire her art. When her old nurse's

The author's favorite bunnies, in a line drawing and two watercolors

son fell ill, Potter wrote to him, "I don't know what to write to you, so I shall tell you a story about four little rabbits," and in this way Flopsy, Mopsy, Cottontail, and Peter came alive on the page. In 1900 she published the story, and Peter Rabbit, in the company of her other beloved characters, has enthralled generations of children ever since.

Potter's home at Sawrey is looked after now by The National Trust. She worked hard to preserve the sweeping beauty of the lakes and left her 4,000 acres in trust for all to enjoy—especially those who stand in her garden and think they just might have seen a rabbit in a powder blue jacket with big brass buttons hopping across the grass.

THE NATURAL WORLD IN MINIATURE

A contemporary artist keeping alive something of Beatrix Potter's sensibility is watercolorist Sara Midda. Her art, like Potter's, is all about close observation and careful rendering. Her paintings are miniature masterpieces, and anyone looking at them could easily imagine that she lives overlooking a well-tended garden with a patchwork vista of fields and meadows stretching into the distance. The truth is that she lives in a tiny London townhouse with a small terrace out back and boxes of herbs her only garden. Nevertheless, she has earnestly researched every leaf, tendril, and aphorism of her subjects, and it is her loving eye that lends her work (which has been gathered together in two delightful volumes) its delicate and detailed charm.

Despite their enchantingly effortless appearance, these are carefully wrought works, for Midda practices her craft with great skill, and selects her subjects carefully. "Cultivated flowers are beautiful and full of color, but they cannot compare in the least with radishes, a pear, or a head of lettuce," she says. In her world, the bright red orb of a radish is as beautiful as a rose, and spinach leaves are limned in tiny accuracy for a beauty that is as scrupulous as it is luminous.

ROMANCE

To think of England is to summon up cottages snug in rose-strewn gardens, or a

rolling vista of fields and meadows, woods and dells. These visions are more

than pretty. They touch the heart, which sees the beauty that history brings—in

the richness of lives lived where countryside and people are forever intertwined.

No frivolous dalliance here; this is where the heart dwells.

A misty morning in Yorkshire

Time for Tea

"IN NOTHING IS THE ENGLISH GENIUS FOR DOMESTICITY MORE NOTABLY declared than in the institution of this festival—almost one may call it so—of afternoon tea. . . . The mere chink of cups and saucers tunes the mind to happy repose," wrote George Gissing in *The Private Papers of Henry Ryecroft*. It was an eighteenth-century Duchess of Bedford who began the tradition. She would order tea to be brewed to revive her flagging spirits whenever she felt a "sinking sensation" in the late afternoon, and eventually began inviting friends to share the pot, a few tidbits and a little gossip, and an institution was born.

Whether a grand celebration or a humble meeting of two friends at the kitchen table, tea with a little something remains an important part of English daily life. At about four or

Fine English bone china, opposite, enhances teatime at a Kew Gardens tea room

. . . half-past four at Manderley, and the table drawn before the library fire . . . the silver tray, the kettle, the snowy cloth.

DAPHNE DU MAURIER

BREWING A PERFECT POT OF TEA

Two things matter when it comes to brewing a perfect cup of tea: the quality of the tea leaves and the teapot. Tea does not keep forever, so buy a tin of good-quality loose leaves at regular intervals, and be sure to store them in an airtight container. The quality of the tea you buy won't count for much, however, if you don't have a proper pot. Pottery, china, or silver are best; avoid aluminum or worn-away enamel on metal, which will taint the taste.

To brew the tea, fill a kettle with freshly drawn cold water and bring to a boil. Remove the kettle from the heat as soon as the water comes to a full boil—oxygen is lost as water boils, thus altering the taste of the water. Warm the pot by rinsing it with a little bit of the boiling water (as the purists do); add the tea—one spoonful for each person, plus one for the pot—fill the pot with water, and put on the lid. Allow the tea to steep for about five minutes, to release the flavor of the leaves. Some teas, such as a delicate Lapsang Souchong, require a shorter steeping time, while a heartier tea, such as an Oolong, will need just a little bit longer. When it's ready to pour, agitate the tea—by stirring it, or simply rotating the pot.

half past, the kettle is put on to boil and the pot prepared. As the shadows lengthen, drivers in Cornwall will make a sharp turn if they see a hand-lettered sign promising "cream teas," for they know that their beverage will be partnered by scones topped with

homemade jam and rich, unctuous Cornish cream. As the church bells chime the hour, shoppers sinking under the weight of bags and baskets slip into a tearoom for a moment of rest and respite, and a delicious piece of pastry.

Tea shops abound in England—every town and village has one, perhaps two—and some, like Sally Lunn's in Bath have been serving to visitors almost as long as tea leaves have been arriving from the Orient.

When tea first appeared in England, in 1657, traders watched in amusement as the proud purchasers stewed the tea leaves in cold water, then spread the dripping mass on slices of bread. It took a little education to learn how to enjoy this fashionable new treat.

In those early days, tea was so costly and rare that it was a luxury solely of the aristocracy. The expensive brew demanded the very finest materials, with a solid silver teapot taking pride of place on the grandest tea tables. It's hardly surprising, therefore, that some of the best in English craftsmanship has been devoted to enhanc-

ing and improving this tradition. Even today artists continue to experiment with the traditional teapot form.

As every collector knows, pots can be found in an astounding variety of shapes—a simple neoclassical form from the early part of the nineteenth century; a furbelowed bulge from the middle of the last century; a sleek deco silhouette from fifty years ago. But for most of us, it is the homely pottery pot that we cherish.

As dusk approaches, we reach into the cupboard for the enduring "Brown Betty"—fat-bellied and made in every size from tea-for-one to tea-for-all-the-family. Because teatime has become family time, this is the hour when little children have their suppers, with bread and butter and sausages (and fairy cakes on a special day), while Mother and elder siblings drink their tea and talk about the events of the day.

And in every good home a battered tin, filled with plain little biscuits—ginger nuts or shortbread or digestives—is always on hand when a friend drops by for tea and a chat, at any time of day.

Where the Heart Comes Home

IF THERE'S A SIGHT THAT DRAWS A SIGH OF COVETOUSNESS, IT SURELY

is the English country cottage. Turn the corner of a country lane, and there it sits, snared in

roses, its garden a whirl of joyous color and profusion, its roofline topped with crooked chim-

neys, tiny windows framing an idyll. Life in a cottage such as this could only be an earthly

paradise.

Originally, of course, it was no such thing. These perfectly formed houses were built as

laborers' cottages and sheltered the large families of workers from medieval days right through

to modern times. Often a date above a doorway or initials carved into a lintel will place

the house in the stream of history, even if the small windows, low ceilings, uneven

In the Cotswolds, a classic cottage entrance, opposite, and its sitting room

Who ever loved,

that loved not

at first sight?

CHRISTOPHER MARLOWE

REVIVING AN ANCIENT ART

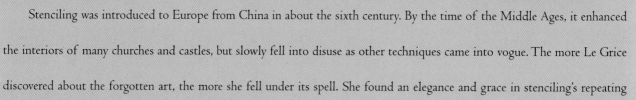

Interior designer Lyn Le Grice is an imaginative, hands-on type of decorator. When she was searching for something new and original to add extra interest to painted walls, she stumbled upon an ancient decorating technique—the art of stenciling.

Stenciling was introduced to Europe from China in about the sixth century. By the time of the Middle Ages, it enhanced the interiors of many churches and castles, but slowly fell into disuse as other techniques came into vogue. The more Le Grice discovered about the forgotten art, the more she fell under its spell. She found an elegance and grace in stenciling's repeating designs, and in short order had created a full-scale revival. Le Grice used her own house in Penzance, Cornwall, as an experimental canvas; after completing the decoration of all seventeen of its rooms, she renamed it "Stencil House" and opened its doors to a mass of eager visitors curious to see the transformation that could be achieved so easily with stencils. It didn't take long to convince many that all a blank wall needs is, say, a sprightly top-knot of flowers dabbed on in an afternoon, or perhaps a regal ribbon motif to thread together the elements of a room.

Fine chintzes and china brighten a cottage living room

floorboards, and rambling staircases don't give enough clues of their own. Most of these little houses were "tied cottages," linked to a landowner's estate and reserved for his workers, or for retired servants from the manor house, or the village schoolmaster, perhaps.

Found throughout England—tucked in at the edge of a Lake District fell, scattered over the gentle hills of Hardy's Dorset, huddled beside the sea in Cornwall—today cottages are the most prized of any dwelling. Each region has its own distinctive character-

istics. The creamy stone of the Cotswolds, for instance, gives villages in Gloucestershire a very different air from Suffolk, where Tudor-framed, half-timbered cottages prevail.

Inside, the inhabitants cherish the evidence of the past and the hard-working lives of the previous occupants. Fireplaces—once the sole source of heat—can still be found in every room, providing warmth and comfort of another kind as well. The kitchen probably still has a flagstone floor and a well-scrubbed work table. In place of

A cottage's cozy jumble of patterns

the long-gone range, there will inevitably be an Aga, an oil-stoked stove that gives constant warmth and heats the water, too. There will be thick stone walls that lend a window a lovely deep sill, low enough for sitting, and mullioned panes to temper the light. Rooms are bound to be small, as these were humble houses, but what an owner gives up in grandeur and spacious proportion is more than made up for in coziness and intimacy.

When it comes to furnishing an English cottage, all must be happily haphazard, a profusion of pattern and color that looks as if everything came together by serendipitous good fortune, which of course it did. In fact, true cottage style resembles a true cottage garden in its chaotic and colorful jumble: A tiny melting pot of textures, colors, and pattern tumbling over pattern—china, embroidered pillows, patchwork quilts, blowsy chintzes, checkered tablecloths, and tartan rugs. Anything and everything, just so long as it's not too big. Each element must be small enough, so that one does not overwhelm another. Then all will be well in this little corner of the world.

BEGUILING WINDOW BOXES

In England, blossoms are everywhere, encouraged by the constant rainy waterings and the mild climate. So beloved are these blooms that many people, not content with just a garden, cast their sights on window ledges as well. Planted anew each season, window boxes make a proud display as they grow in happy profusion—a medley of colors that cheer the heart.

Successful window-box gardening depends on good drainage; boxes must have holes in the bottom, covered by a layer of gravel or stones, before the planting medium is added. A regular dose of plant food will keep the plants in top condition. Classic window-box choices include geraniums, petunias, lobelia, heliotropes, and dahlias; more experimental gardeners might look to Persian violets, African daisies, celosia, or even ornamental peppers.

Brimming with vibrant color and perhaps providing an eye-catching contrast to painted shutters, window boxes, and their close relation, hanging baskets, are irresistible. When placed beside a door, they create a welcome so cheery, one cannot help but be beguiled.

Gardens of Scent and Sight

"AMONG THE MANY THINGS MADE BY MAN NOTHING IS PRETTIER than an English cottage garden. The absence of any pretentious 'plan' . . . lets the flowers tell their story to the heart," wrote Victorian horticulturist William Robinson in 1898, describing the garden that, more than any other, tugs at our heartstrings and gives us a sense of ease. The cottage garden is a matter of scent as well as sight, its sweet tumbling disorder making it all seem joyfully accessible and inviting.

Cottage gardens originated many centuries ago when villagers planted tiny plots outside their doors with the vegetables they needed and the flowers they loved—by happy accident creating a mingling of sense and sensibility, so that a clump of chives, with its

Blooming beauties in the garden at Snape Cottage in Dorset

And cottage-gardens
smelling everywhere,
Confused with smell
of orchards.

ELIZABETH BARRETT
BROWNING

seemingly artless combination of shape, color, and scent that more rigid attentions discourage, and which those early cottage gardeners achieved with such little obvious effort. This is not the place for straight rows, or segregated colors, or strict plantings. Though you probably won't find cabbages nestling beneath the rose bushes, you may see an underplanting of wild flowers or sweet herbs, or even a visitor that in another place might be considered a weed, but is prized here for its fragrance or its subtle coloration.

The essence of a cottage garden is always profusion—the peonies that pour forth in spring, the pinks that send their sharp scent through the air, the poppies that dance along the wall. Such gardens are planted in any spare bit of earth—lining a fence or wall, curving round a path, laid out in a tiny patch beside an entrance door where it becomes part of the welcome.

In such a garden butterflies will flutter round the lavender and lilac, and a trip outdoors to cut herbs for dinner is enriched by the beautiful blooms of the flowering shrubs that

lavender-colored blossoms, could shake its round heads beside an unfolding rose. Tousled and tangled and full to the brim these original cottage gardens were. In any of these crowded patches your eye might have caught careless banners of honeysuckle cascading over the fences that surrounded them, or clematis winding its way around nearby windows, while strawberries might have bobbed at the edge of the path near carrots and lettuces marching in rows beneath the first roses.

You still might glimpse such charming chaos, because many of the gardens that framed the pretty cottages still exist, or have been recreated. And so well loved was the style that soon it was imitated by owners of much grander plots, who were captivated by the happy informality of the plantings and who would set aside a portion of their own gardens in which to emulate the glorious abundance.

Now we think of almost any intermingling of pattern and plant as a "cottage garden," and many seek the

Lush gardens at Sleightholmedale Lodge in Yorkshire, opposite and above

The Vegetable Patch

Is there anything more ordinary than a vegetable? And yet, fresh and crisp, is there anything more glorious? Even the process of picking is a pleasure, where a tug on a topknot yields a golden carrot, a browse through chard leads to a visual feast—sharp green, vivid red. It's tempting to linger even if not in search of beans for dinner. But beyond a pleasure for the senses, the patch should be practically planned, to provide food for the household all year round.

A potager (Old English for the part of a garden that supplies the potage, or soup pot) was customarily placed just outside the kitchen door. But in 1620 Sir Francis Bacon advised a square garden "within which are to be little low hedges," to make the interior accessible. William Lawson, a seventeenth-century Yorkshire clergyman, further suggested that if each square were cut into smaller squares "none more than five feet across," it would be all the better for weeding.

After laying the garden out, ample planting softens the geometry, with color and form a matter of contrast. Blue cabbages pop their round heads up near the leek blossoms, and golden shrubs contrast with green. Vegetable gardens are abundance writ large, and here there is plenty in the produce, and in the effect. The joy of such a garden lies in discovery, of the next growing season and all its promise.

surround the patch. Those who want to stray down the path and not return for a while will find pretty gates and fences, inviting arbors, and secret garden seats.

Happily, the new interest in cottage gardens has revived the planting of long-forgotten perennials and herbs, and old-fashioned roses. Now there is a feast of heirloom choices for the garden—towering hollyhocks, primroses, columbines, love-in-a-mist, and daisies can mingle. Borders containing lady's mantel and fennel mark paths, and special scent gardens play with the aromas of sage, mint, and lemon balm, sending a fountain of sweet fragrance into the air.

The star in all the delightful chaos, however, is the rose. Whether rambling along a fence, planted in a border, or clambering up the cottage walls, roses demand—prettily, nicely, but without hesitation—to be the centerpiece.

Lucky indeed is the owner of such a garden—but lucky, too, are those who round a corner in a lane and come across such glorious disarray.

For the Love of the Rose

"I WILL MAKE THEE BEDS OF ROSES AND A THOUSAND FRAGRANT POSIES," wrote Christopher Marlowe in his poem "The Passionate Shepherd to His Love." If ever there was a flower that spoke of love, then surely it is the rose. But roses are also the very symbol of England—turn over the coin of the realm, and there they are. It's hard to imagine England without envisioning a tangle of them around a cottage door. Even so, though the flower's dominion on Earth is older even than man's, it is believed that roses only arrived in England when they were brought home by Crusaders to the Holy Land sometime during the eleventh, twelfth, and thirteenth centuries.

It was monks who first cultivated rose bushes in monastery gardens, primarily for

Roses bloom at Cleveland House in East Sussex

What's in a name?
that which we call a rose,
By any other name
would smell as sweet . . .

WILLIAM SHAKESPEARE

Roses from the Round House in Surrey, above, and Hadspen House in Somerset, opposite

medicinal use—copying the Persians, who had discovered ages before that rose oil could be used to cure all kinds of ailments. But it wasn't long before those who loved the rose began to cross-breed the many varieties growing so abundantly in their gardens. As modern growers still do today, the medieval plantsmen sought the ultimate rose by combining the best in terms of color, scent, and form from the blowsy, many-petaled early varieties with their evocative names—the Damask, the Alba, the Gallicas.

Unfortunately, so successful were the newly developed roses, and so popular, that as time went on the old-fashioned roses began to disappear—until, that is, rose detectives, scouring old garden sites and deserted dooryards, began to collect and raise the remnants of England's heritage roses.

By the 1950s a large collection of rescued old-fashioned roses was available for rose-lovers to choose from and combine with their hybrid teas and modern shrubs.

Given the misty English weather that encourages their luxuriant growth, it's little wonder that a multitude of roses lies at the heart of the English garden. Even the smallest plot will have a climbing rose flinging flowers across the gate, or an arbor lifting aloft a burden of blossoms that sweeten the air. Roses of all sorts and colors are mixed, providing a patchwork of color.

Those in pursuit of a profusion of roses and wealth of rose knowledge might want to visit the Royal National Rose Society's garden at St. Albans in Hertfordshire. There rosarians can see the rainbow of varieties gathered together since the society's founding in 1976.

Surely the heart of England lies in the rose. This most beloved flower is used in metaphor throughout the English language—in prose, poem, and song. In *The Faerie Queene*, for example, Edmund Spencer allegorized his queen, Elizabeth I, writing—

Gather therefore the Rose, whilst yet is prime,
For soon comes age, that will her pride deflower:
Gather the Rose of love whilst yet is time.

And what is a beautiful English girl called? An English rose, of course.

ROSES IN THE NAME OF DESIGN

For Mary Rose Young, a rose is much more than simply the beautiful flower her mother named her after. An imaginative and experimental artist and designer, Mary Rose uses the image of the rose to create many of her stunning motifs. She finds inspiration not just in the flower, but in its patterns and shapes—the juxtaposition of leaf to bloom, the way the petals unfold, the majesty of the blossom—all glorious and decorative designs to doodle and starting points for her improvisation.

The result is witty and vividly colored pottery pieces, such as those shown here, which are typical of Young's artistic approach—covered as they are with lighthearted renderings that ramble and roam. They bring to mind the decorative art produced by the artists of the Bloomsbury group at Charleston Farmhouse, Vanessa Bell's Sussex home, in the early part of the twentieth century.

The rose has found its way into the decor of Young's shop in Bath and into her own home; both burst with color and pattern, embellished with roses and squiggles that seem spontaneous, and usually are. "If something is slightly wonky, it has more life," she says, with little patience for precision. Because Young's art is never serious, her credo couldn't be more straightforward: "If you can paint a simple doodle, that's as much as you can expect a design to be."

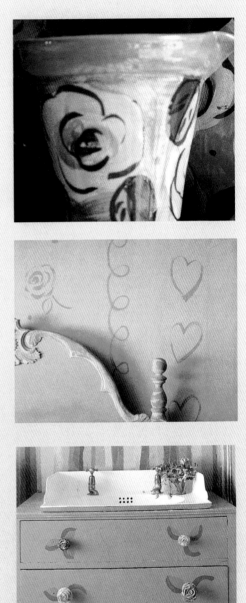

Where Passions Burned

SURPRISING AS THE FLOWERS THAT FIND THEIR WAY IN WILD AND windswept places are the works wrought by the Brontë sisters—Charlotte, Emily, and Anne—whose short lives unfolded in a small household set in the vastness of the Yorkshire landscape.

But our contemporary minds have trouble grasping what it must have been like to grow up as the Brontë children did—in a cold stone house in Haworth where tombstones in the churchyard marched right up to the windowsill. For its time, the framework of their lives was not an uncommon one, filled as it was with death, domesticity, and duty. Among their earliest memories must surely have been the sound of weeping, as first their mother was carried off to her grave, then their elder sisters, Maria and Elizabeth. A silence must have descended

Wandering the remote Yorkshire moors in the footsteps of the Brontës

*Because the road is
rough and long,
Shall we despise the
skylark's song?*

ANNE BRONTË

At the Brontës' home in Haworth, scenes from parsonage life: stairs made of Yorkshire stone, above; a bedroom, opposite top; and the grandfather clock, opposite bottom

Keeper, their dog, at their heels. At night, they talked and talked, and spun vivid tales. They had a set of toy soldiers, which their childish imaginations turned into characters with which to people the stories they wrote. Their spider writing filled tiny handmade books as they created fanciful worlds that blended news of war and heroes from the outside world with the fantastic plots of the novels they loved to read.

As they grew older, each sister made a journey or two away from home—to work as a governess, to learn French in Brussels—but was always drawn to return to the rugged village of Haworth to resume domestic family life in the chilly parsonage.

It wasn't until 1846, when Charlotte discovered Emily's poems, that the sisters thought of publishing their poetry and stories. They gathered together their writings and released them privately—to critical silence.

Undeterred, the sisters then began writing novels. Charlotte, Emily, and Anne each had a story close to her heart that wove the reali-

upon the house, as their father, a solitary man by temperament, sat in his study composing his sermons.

The surviving children—the three sisters and their brother, Branwell—were left to entertain themselves. They became everything to one another. By day, they strode the moors, with

ties of their lives with flights of imagination. Death and despair, the beauty of the moors, the wild heart's longing—they may have been three women in drab dresses, but beneath the quiet exteriors, passions burned. It was William Thackeray who said of Charlotte, "There's a fire raging in that little woman."

Finally the manuscripts were sent to a publisher, the precious packet marked with the male pseudonyms each had derived from her initial—Currer, Ellis, and Acton Bell. All three novels were published in 1847—Charlotte's *Jane Eyre*, Anne's *Agnes Grey*, and Emily's *Wuthering Heights*—amid great speculation. Who were the true authors of these novels that so transcended Victorian conventions?

Emily died at age thirty, before the furor about her book reached her; and Anne passed away six months later, at twenty-nine. Charlotte was left alone, Keeper lying at her feet, the "hard frost and keen wind" plucking at her, her father sequestered in his study. For a few years she was lionized in London, and the first of the literary

pilgrims clamored to meet her. But in 1855, at age thirty-eight and not long after she'd married her father's curate, she, too, fell to the tuberculosis that had claimed the others' lives.

Her father lived on among his papers for many years, courteously receiving visitors who came to marvel

at the simple setting where genius had stirred. Today the old village church honors the family with a plaque, and each year thousands of people crowd into the little churchyard and walk the steep streets of Haworth.

Many also venture down the signposted paths that lead onto the moors, and so follow in the footsteps of the Brontë sisters. The landscape around the village threads through all of their novels. For these three women, who lived lives constricted by duty, found freedom in their passionate imaginations, and in the wild sweep of land and sky that lay about them.

I sought, and soon discovered, the three
head-stones on the slope next to the moor—
the middle one, grey, and half buried in
heath—Edgar Linton's only harmonized by
the turf, and moss creeping up its foot—
Heathcliff's still bare.

I lingered round them, under that benign
sky; watched the moths fluttering among the
heath, and hare-bells; listened to the soft
wind breathing through the grass; and
wondered how any one could ever imagine
unquiet slumbers, for the sleepers in that
quiet earth.

Emily Brontë

Wuthering Heights

Pride of Place

English pride has little to do with flag-waving. You have to look for subtler signs,

such as tending the roses around the front door to ensure blossoms will continue

to cascade, and knowing that glittering boots and brass bands will forever accom-

pany the pomp and circumstance of royal pageantry. Where history lies behind

every hedgerow, the pride lies in the vow: There will always be an England.

A field of rape seed

The Sigh of the Sea

"ENGLAND, BOUND IN WITH THE TRIUMPHANT SEA, WHOSE ROCKY shore beats back the envious siege, Of watery Neptune . . . " So wrote William Shakespeare for his play *Richard II*, words that begin to explain the English fascination with the sea. There she lies like a bright green emerald, with waves dashing silver all around, so that an Englishman's or Englishwoman's sense of the sea is never far away. The sea shifts and sighs, thunders in a storm, or whispers on a gentle sunstruck day, its wild freedom an antidote to lives spent enclosed by hills, in villages hidden in every turn and bend of the road. Those who hunger for the sensation of wide horizons and swift breezes, of boats that dip and sway against the skyline, of golden stretches of sand lapping at the foot of cliffs, can drive

On the Isles of Scilly, thrift grows at the sea's edge, opposite, and a mast rises high

This happy breed of men, this little world, This precious stone set in the silver sea . . .

WILLIAM SHAKESPEARE

away, returning many years later with ships full of treasure and heads full of tales of all they'd seen.

Seldom can those adventures have been quite so dramatic or horrific as those related by the Ancient Mariner in Samuel Taylor Coleridge's epic poem, *The Rhyme of the Ancient Mariner*, but it's not hard to understand the undercurrent of exhilaration that must have accompanied those brave adventurers as they traveled to places and oceans brand new to the map of the world:

The fair breeze blew, the white foam flew,
The furrow followed free:
We were the first that ever burst
Into that silent sea.

The sea showed the way to dreamers as well as to fortune-seekers, and it pointed out a new direction to those who could not find a place in England. These searchers packed their trunks and followed the compass west or south, settling in faraway lands to begin another life.

Today the sea beckons as strongly as ever. At Royal Cowes each August, and at other regattas around the country,

In Devon, a street in the seaside town of Dartmouth, above, and a cat relaxing on the beach at Clovelly

an hour or two, and there survey the crashing waves and feel the beat of the wind upon their face.

Until a hundred years ago, however, the sea was a highway, its siren call a summons to explorers and adventurers who would pull up anchor and sail

ROSAMUND PILCHER

The sea sounds through many of the stories written by Rosamund Pilcher, whose best-selling novels of life and love have entranced readers all over the world. And yet, in many ways, Pilcher couldn't be a more local author, for she returns again and again in her stories to the Cornwall coast where she lived as a girl. Books such as *The Shell Seekers* and *Coming Home* are filled with the boom of the waves, the shoreline's pull, and the sea that reflects the sky's mood, whether cloudy or bright. Here, Pilcher the storyteller is at home, a close observer of the ways of the little villages that are tucked along the coast, the interweaving of families and daily life that remained unchanged until well after World War II.

She began to write seriously after her four children were born, plunking a typewriter onto the kitchen table and working as they played nearby. Though she carefully researches the history behind her stories, Pilcher finds her true material in the workings of the human heart, weaving local characters into her novels: "Mrs. Berry, who ran the village shop and made her own ice-creams out of custard powder . . . and Mrs. Southey in the post office, who set a fire-guard on the counter to keep bandits at bay . . . . " "I knew the stories of people's lives," she says. And surely, therein, lies the novelist's art.

the great yachts yaw and come about, and the pennants whip in the wind. All along the coast dinghies and small boats ply, and each successive generation of children learns the joys of boats and of boating, because, in the words of Ratty in Kenneth Grahame's classic book *The Wind in the Willows,* "There is nothing—absolutely nothing—half so much worth doing as simply messing about in boats . . . or with boats. . . . In or out of 'em, it doesn't matter."

Grahame is in excellent company. English writers have always turned their faces to the sea for that sense of place which illuminates so much of their work. Grahame loved the small Cornwall town of Fowey, as did Daphne du Maurier, who made it her home. Its proximity to water captivated her. "Down the harbour, round the point, was the open sea. Here was the freedom I desired, long sought for, not yet known. Freedom to write, to walk, to wander, freedom to climb hills, to pull a boat, to be alone."

So beloved was the sea to du Maurier that in books like *Rebecca* and *Frenchman's Creek* it almost becomes another character, signaling changes of mood, menacing or mirthful. For du Maurier, pacing the clifftops that overlooked the sea was an important part of the creative process—she even had a little hut built, perched above the sea, where she could sit and think and pen the stories beloved by so many readers.

But it is poets who often seem best able to capture the sweep of the sea, the washing of the waves providing the meter to their measures. The lyrical undulations of John Masefield's *Sea Fever* illustrate the ocean's pull.

I must go down to the seas again,
*   to the lonely sea and the sky,*
And all I ask is a tall ship and a star
*   to steer her by,*
And the wheel's kick and the wind's song
*   and the white sail's shaking,*
And a gray mist on the sea's face and
*   a gray dawn breaking.*

I must go down to the seas again, for the
*   call of the running tide*
Is a wild call and a clear call that may
*   not be denied.*

Ruined engine houses in Cornwall, opposite, and a wall on the Isles of Scilly, above

This Green and Pleasant Land

ENGLAND REMAINS PROFOUNDLY CAUGHT UP IN THE ROMANCE OF

the rural, even as her cities hum and her countryside empties of people truly country-bred. A

deeply embedded sense remains etched in the English consciousness that though city life may

be all very well, it's only in the country that one's real life is lived. The belief can be glimpsed

in that insistent cry to every child: "Go outside and get some air," in the stream of cars head-

ing out of London every Friday night, occupants willing to fight the traffic for a brief rural

reverie, and in the sudden appearance of country clothes on London's streets whenever rain

clouds roll in. Modern England's love of the outdoors expresses itself first as a matter of

style. Just watch the waxed coats and wellie boots go clomping by, as if the wearer were off

The essentials of country life, opposite, for exploring around a woodland bridge

Hills, vales, woods,
netted in a silver mist,
Farms, granges, doubled
up among the hills . . .

ELIZABETH
BARRETT BROWNING

to the stable instead of riding to work on the underground.

Carrying on no matter what the weather might be is paramount, and defines English dress, in some ways even the very personality of its people. The practicalities of forging ahead have made an art form of country clothes: layers of warm woolies and quilted waistcoats, jackets with plenty of pockets, canvas fishing bags and hats of various persuasions—the sort of clothing that has an evocative smell, from age and from the saddle soap and wax required to maintain its waterproofness. Piece by piece, these are accumulated and passed from generation to generation.

It's not all about dressing up in the right kind of clothes, however. The call of the countryside is strong, and the English can't help but listen. The land and its people are inextricably linked. This island, with its borders that define and limit where one can go, has been cultivated by the English people for eons. To a large degree, it's hard to escape the sense that over time they've made the countryside what it

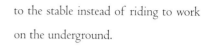

Pursuing favorite pastimes in the English countryside, above and opposite

is, by farming, by landscaping parkland around the great mansions and palaces, such as Bleinhem and Stowe, by planting forests and woods—and, conversely, by cutting them down (to make the ships that formed the great navy which was once England's pride).

Deep delight comes from this harmonious, sculpted landscape, from the way the hedgerows tuck in the fields and the villages scarcely interrupt the long roll of hills on the way to the sea. At counterpoint is just as deep a respect for the untamed parts of the country: the Lake District, Dartmoor, the Yorkshire moors. Such sensibilities, and the fact that the historical is never too far off, mean that even the activities and sports which occupy a country person's time, when work is done, carry with them a link to the past and a strong sense of tradition.

One such activity is hunting, a ritual that scatters dogs and horses and humans across the countryside. Beauty can be found in its forms: the red coats flashing by, the mahogany and chestnut horses arching over a brook. "The unspeakable in pursuit of the inedible," say those who find the sport off-putting. But for many, this is tradition to the core, an established, generations-old way of uniting people with the land they inhabit.

Like hunting, fishing has drawn people to areas of heartbreaking beauty for centuries; however, it delivers a much more tranquil experience. Some of fishing's appeal comes from the balance of patience and skill it demands; other people delight in its arcane equipment, refined only slightly over the years.

Anglers cultivate control and savor solitude as they find a silent stretch of a river or row across a lake. Catch nothing? No matter, there are compensations, like lunch from a wicker basket (smoked salmon sandwiches nibbled under a pine tree) while the wind softly sings.

Picnicking has always been a favorite English pastime. And a totally nonsensical one it is, too, when you

can't trust the weather (but then, you see, they've got the clothing all worked out, so a few raindrops, even a downpour, won't be too disheartening). This passion has to do with optimism; and there is something beguiling about the preparations. So much of the English character is about hoping for the best, and when the best doesn't quite come up to scratch, making the most of it anyway. Disappointed picnickers can always decamp to the pub, preferably one with an excellent home-brew on tap.

The Charm of China

THE POTTERS OF TODAY ARE AS INVENTIVE AS ANY ENGLAND HAS enjoyed, and fortunately there's always demand for a flowerpot or an egg cup, a plate or a teapot. Although the chinawares from the Staffordshire potteries—from the likes of Spode and Minton, Royal Doulton and Wedgwood—are still well loved, the fresh eyes of contemporary craftspeople are bringing new vision to old forms.

One form whose popularity has risen, fallen, and then risen again according to the vagaries of style is the combination of blue and white. In the earliest days of china production, the cheerfully painted blue and white "delftware" made in Holland was so wildly popular in England that English manufacturers soon began to produce their

The art of Isis Ceramics in Oxford, opposite, and ceramic lids before painting

Sincerity in art is not an affair of will. . . . It is mainly an affair of talent.

ALDOUS HUXLEY

love with its simple beauty and charm.

A still-life painter by trade, Sears longed to recreate the lovely (and now much sought after) originals. She devoted four years to the effort, working by trial and error, to rediscover the lost glaze formulas.

Eventually, she was successful. She founded Isis Ceramics in Oxford, now a thriving operation with six painters at work on a wide variety of motifs, borrowed from nature and from noble houses, which are scattered upon plates and platers, bulb pots, teapots, and vases. All the designs are replicas of patterns that date back hundreds of years, and while each of the pieces is unique, a work of art in itself, all live happily together. "It's like two musicians playing the same tune, which is recognizable, but never exactly the same. That's what keeps the works so fresh," says Sears.

own delftware as well. Eventually, of course, fashions changed, other kinds of china came into vogue, and some of the production methods were lost as they fell out of use.

Today, examples of the original seventeenth-century English delftware are rare. When artist Deborah Sears came upon a piece in a London thrift shop, she'd never seen anything quite like it before, despite a life-long interest in china, and she immediately fell in

Another artist, Emma Bridgewater, has also revived an old technique to create her fresh and whimsical pottery. Throughout the nineteenth century, spongeware—its designs stamped with a sponge (or sometimes spattered) onto each piece in bold and colorful patterns—was a much-loved favorite on the tables of humble homes.

Bridgewater brings a contemporary wit and a vibrant palette to the almost-lost technique. But it hasn't been easy for her, either—she had no formal art training, and had to discover how best to cut a natural sea sponge with which to create her delightful designs. Then she needed to locate a factory that could produce unpainted pots and plates for her. But as soon as she printed her first piece, with roses and leaves, she knew she had created "something new and quite wonderful."

Today, Bridgewater runs a thriving business, and besides owning a factory and a shop in London, she recently opened a "pottery café" where visitors can sip tea and stamp patterns on their own pieces. The appeal of china, it seems, is ageless.

Isis Ceramics china and the company's mark, opposite; a teapot by Emma Bridgewater, above

The High Street

WHEN MISS MAPP, IN E. F. BENSON'S COMIC "LUCIA" NOVELS, TOOK UP her basket and headed for the high street in the little town of Tilling, she went out to gather much more than just provisions. With a dawdle here and an eavesdrop there, and a good long chat with the postmistress, she got in touch with all the day's news, all the scandals and comings and goings that thrilled her, as she bought two eggs and a length of embroidery cotton. Benson, whose own hometown of Rye in Sussex is the consummate small town, knew that an hour spent on the high street tapped into everything that made a community.

Certainly a high street had, and indeed still has, all manner of necessities. There's the ironmonger for tools and hardware, the grocer, the baker and the butcher, the newsagent

The & Clarke's bakery in Kensington, opposite, and the high street in Haworth, above

There are so many good shops here. . . . One can step out of doors and get a thing in five minutes.

JANE AUSTEN

housewives skittered from shop to shop, checking their lists against the contents of the baskets swinging from their arms, they'd pause for a friendly chat with passersby, with the greengrocer, or with the ironmonger.

So entrenched in English life is the high street that even London has "villages" with just such streets at their core. The neighborhood of Marylebone, for example, has Marylebone High Street, while the buzzing center in Kensington is Kensington High Street.

To be bought on the high street: potpourri, above; antique lace, right; and flowers, opposite

with the post office in the back of the store, the haberdasher, and the florist.

For hundreds of years, this was it for most shoppers—except for market day each week, when peddlers and salesmen from out of town would set up their stalls in the high street.

High streets had their regional distinctions, too. You'd be able to buy pasties and saffron buns in Cornwall, but nowhere else. And if you wanted a Bakewell tart for supper, you'd better

make certain you were in Derbyshire.

Only the very fortunate ever went beyond the local high street for their purchases. Jane Austen, for example, frequently visited relatives in London, and lived for a short time in Bath, where the haberdasher's counter offered her a wider choice of silks, muslins, and ribbons than she could find in Chawton.

Shopping demanded daily attention, so it's little wonder that it became part of the social life of a town. As

Sally Lunn's teashop in Bath

The rhythms of the day find their echo on high street, too. Children stop in at the sweet shop with a penny for a treat after school, or run to the baker to buy fresh, warm rolls for lunch. And weary shoppers will always find at least one tea shop to sustain them. Wide windows looking out onto the street mean they can enjoy the passing parade as they slice into their cakes. Life is made of these small moments, these little details, and the interweaving of people and place.

Of course, bigger events have had their celebrations here as well. Over the years, high streets have been adorned with bunting and flags for the queen's jubilee, a local fair, or a street party to celebrate a long war's end at last.

As modern life cuts across the English village, the high street is under siege from chain stores and a faster pace of life that leaves little time for window-shopping. Wise residents, however, know they have a treasure in their grasp, and are working hard to preserve the special precinct where commerce and community have always touched.

In towns like the Georgian city of Bath, the traditional shops of the high street mingle with other stores: gift emporiums selling a glorious array of china and glass, boutiques full of up-to-the-minute fashions, antiques shops, and florists. For this is where the future lies—in a melting pot of past and present, locals and visitors from afar.

RITUALS OF VILLAGE LIFE

Take a seat on the village green, shut your eyes, and sense the life around you—in many English towns, the sounds are little changed from those of a hundred years ago. Early in the morning, you'll hear the clink, clink of milk bottles as the milkman makes his rounds, and running steps as children hurry, late again for school. A sharp whistle? That's the man who lives on the corner calling his dog before they head off for a walk. A more tuneful hum comes from the woman who runs the village store as she throws open the shop's shutters. In only a minute the first customers file in, looking for bread, and newspapers just down from London. And so the day unfolds in its accustomed way.

Writers have long known that a village is the perfect setting for a novel. Jane Austen set the example, proving there was much to be made of lives that intertwine as they do in a small setting. But she's in good company—look at Mrs. Gaskell's *Cranford*, or Flora Thompson's *Lark Rise to Candleford*, or the more contemporary Miss Read and Joanna Trollope.

Village rituals are eternal—a church congregation gathers faithfully for evensong, the annual fête fills the manor-house lawns one more time. The Women's Institute rolls along, and there's always someone stopping in at the tea shop, where the scones—and the gossip—are fresh. On summer evenings, when the sun sets late and the light plays across the green, a cricket match unfolds. Time stops; and this is an image that the English, however far from home, hold dear in their hearts.

Of Love and Society

THE HAMPSHIRE VILLAGE OF CHAWTON COULD BE ANYWHERE IN

rural England. Low-roofed houses cluster round the church and everything stops for tea. But

it was here that Jane Austen came in 1809, to the house her brother Edward had made ready

for his sisters and mother. And it was here, in this otherwise unexceptional place, that Austen

made her home and spun stories which looked on the ordinary and turned it into art.

It's easy to see her still, in the graceful, nearly empty spaces of her home, where light

floods the rooms and the lane beyond the front door hums with life, as it's always done.

There's the tea set that Austen had charge of, the portrait her beloved sister, Cassandra,

The writing table at Jane Austen's home, Chawton Cottage in Hampshire

' *And what are you reading, Miss—?' 'Oh! it is only a novel!' replies the young lady . . . with affected indifference.*

JANE AUSTEN

FOR THE LOVE OF SILK

"I've been ruining myself in black satin ribbon," lamented Jane Austen in a letter to a friend, for she was just as susceptible as any woman to fitting herself up for fashion. In her day, that meant a flounce of ruffled taffeta or a length of satin ribbon to trim a bonnet. Happily, just down the road from her home at Chawton was Whitchurch Silk Mill, whose looms produced the glorious stream of finely wrought silk that glowed temptingly at the draper's. Two hundred years later, the mill still operates,

the last of the many silk mills that once clattered away beside English rivers. At Whitchurch, the swift-flowing waters of the River Test continue to drive the looms—as the waterwheel turns, the bobbins spin, the shuttles fly back and forth, and shimmering folds of fabric grow.

Twenty years ago, this was where the silk taffeta for the Princess of Wales's wedding gown was woven. Lawyers who "take silk," after being appointed Queen's Counsel, come here for the twelve yards of black ottoman they need for their robes. Costumers for film and theater looking for authenticity, and museum curators needing snippets to restore vintage gowns—all know this is the place for silken treasures like no other.

painted of her, the quilt all the women of the household pieced together, and the small round table (shown on page 138) she would pull next to the fire after breakfast had been cleared away. Here Austen penned *Persuasion, Mansfield Park*, and *Emma*, writing away on her portable desk in the morning, slipping the papers out of sight whenever the creaking door warned her that visitors approached.

Love and society—these were her subjects, and she found them near at hand and in her own experiences. To think of Jane Austen as a housebound spinster is wrong. She was part of a large, well-read, and energetic family, and constantly off on visits to relatives with grand houses, or on expeditions to London, Bath, and coastal towns such as Sidmouth in Devon. She even found her own romance when she fell in love with a young clergyman, although nothing came of it in the end.

Nevertheless, Austen knew many of the secrets of the heart, as her novels bear testament. And her characters lay just outside the door: "3 or 4 families in a Country Village is the very thing to

A Jane Austen dress

work on," she wrote in a letter in 1814.

The world discovered her after the publication of *Sense and Sensibility* in 1811 (although she wrote it many years earlier, in 1798). Even the Prince Regent expressed his curiosity about the author, who has become one of the most beloved in the English canon, with her stories wrought from the small details of life.

With more than usual eagerness did Catherine hasten to the Pumproom the next day, secure within herself of seeing Mr. Tilney there before the morning were over, and ready to meet him with a smile:—but no smile was demanded—Mr. Tilney did not appear. Every creature in Bath, except himself, was to be seen in the room at different periods of the fashionable hours; crowds of people were every moment passing in and out, up the steps and down; people whom nobody cared about, and nobody wanted to see; and he only was absent. "What a delightful place Bath is," said Mrs. Allen, as they sat down near the great clock, after parading the room till they were tired; "and how pleasant it would be if we had any acquaintance here."

JANE AUSTEN
Northanger Abbey

Le Manoir aux Quat' Saisons in Oxford

AFTERWORD

Victoria has always felt at home in the soft rolling hills, green lawns, and bright and shining seacoasts of England. Each year we travel to these places in one special issue. We have walked the Lake District in the footsteps of Wordsworth and politely tarried in Jane Austen's home. And we have found the heart of England—in the people we have met in this country where creativity continues to flourish. You can be treetop in a folly, you can be in a knee-high village and garden just for children. Artisans abound in this land of letters; and we marvel that we never seem to run out of fascinating stories.

For all who have come along in this book, we feel that you have been jolly companions in the same search—to discover anew that there is so much to see and learn. Of course we could all stay in the joy of an English garden forever. Or take tea on an afternoon in a tidy town where time does stand still. This book we hope has given you the desire to see more of England—so we encourage you to travel there soon with *The Heart of England* as your guide.

Nancy Lindemeyer

TRADITIONAL ENGLISH RECIPES

Sarah Meade's fruitcakes

A SAVORY TRADITION

The Victorians and Edwardians gloried in their dinners. These were rich feasts where course after course appeared on the table, of contrasting flavors chosen by the lady of the house in close consultation with the cook. One souvenir of those long-gone days, when soup began the meal and fish was always present, is the savory course. Designed literally to be savored, these are tempting, sharp-flavored tidbits that were served after the main course as palate-cleansing preludes to dessert. Nowadays, we might choose one of these little treats as a lunch in itself or as a tasty companion to port, claret, or even tea.

The origin of the name "Angels and Devils on Horseback" is uncertain, but English food historian Michelle Berriedale-Johnson believes it would have been just the sort of thing to be featured in a P. G. Wodehouse novel. A favorite of the Victorians was Stilton, Pear, and Watercress Savory, and Samuel Pepys, way back in the seventeenth century, raved about The Bacon and Almond Tart.

Note: A metric conversion chart can be found on page 163.

ANGELS AND DEVILS ON HORSEBACK

8 FRESH OYSTERS, CLAMS, OR MUSSELS
    (FOR THE "ANGELS")
8 PITTED PRUNES, CHICKEN LIVERS, OR MUSHROOMS
    (FOR THE "DEVILS")
8 SLICES BACON, HALVED CROSSWISE
RED LEAF LETTUCE
4 SLICES TOASTED WHITE BREAD, HALVED, FOR GARNISH

1. Preheat the oven to 350°F. Wrap each oyster in a half slice of bacon and secure with wooden picks. Wrap each prune in a half slice of bacon and secure with wooden picks. Arrange the "angels" and "devils" in a shallow baking pan.

2. Bake for 15 to 20 minutes, until the bacon is crisp but the fillings are still moist.

3. To serve, arrange the savories on a bed of lettuce and remove the wooden picks. Garnish with the toast.

Yield: 4 servings

SAMUEL PEPYS'S BACON AND ALMOND TART

> ¾ CUP UNBLEACHED FLOUR
> ½ CUP WHOLE-WHEAT PASTRY FLOUR
> ICE WATER
> 6 TABLESPOONS COLD UNSALTED BUTTER, CUT INTO
>   BITS
> ½ POUND BACON
> 1¼ CUPS SLIVERED ALMONDS, GROUND
> 2½ TABLESPOONS SUPERFINE SUGAR
> 2 TEASPOONS ROSE WATER
> PESTICIDE-FREE STRAWBERRY LEAVES
>   AND PINK FLOWERS, FOR GARNISH

1. In a medium-size bowl, combine both the flours. With a pastry blender or two knives, cut in the butter until the mixture resembles a very coarse meal.

2. Gradually sprinkle 4 to 5 tablespoons ice water over the flour mixture, tossing with a fork until moistened. Shape the dough into a ball, then wrap in plastic and refrigerate for 30 minutes.

3. Roll out the dough on a lightly floured surface. Fit it into a 7-inch pie plate, flute the edge, and prick all over with a fork. Line the pastry shell with foil and fill the foil with pie weights. Freeze for 30 minutes. Preheat the oven to 450°F.

4. Bake the pastry shell for 10 to 12 minutes, until lightly brown. Remove the foil and weights, and cool the pastry shell on a rack.

5. Arrange the bacon on a rack in a shallow baking pan. Bake for 12 to 14 minutes, until just beginning to crisp. Drain the bacon on paper towels, then cut into ½-inch pieces.

6. Reduce the oven temperature to 350°F.

7. In a large bowl, combine the almonds, sugar, and rose water, and mix well. Stir in the bacon and spoon the mixture into the cooled pastry shell.

8. Bake the tart for 25 to 30 minutes, until the bacon is crisp.

9. Serve the tart warm or at room temperature, garnished with strawberry leaves and pink flowers.

Yield: 4 servings

STILTON, PEAR, AND WATERCRESS SAVORY

> 4 SLICES TOASTED DARK RYE BREAD
> 1 LARGE BUNCH WATERCRESS,
>   TORN INTO SMALL SPRIGS
> 2 PEARS, PEELED, CORED, AND SLICED
> 8 OUNCES STILTON CHEESE, CRUMBLED
> BLACK PEPPER
> RED LEAF LETTUCE

1. Preheat the oven to 400°F.

2. Arrange the toast in a shallow baking pan and layer half of the watercress, then half of the pear slices over the toast. Repeat this process with the remaining watercress and pear slices. Sprinkle the Stilton over the top layer of pears.

3. Bake for 10 to 12 minutes, until the cheese is melted and bubbling. Remove the baking dish from the oven and let rest for 5 minutes.

4. Grind the pepper over the savory. Slice and serve on plates lined with the lettuce.

Yield: 4 servings

ON THE TEA TABLE

Teatime in England could never be complete without these staples: crumpets, preferably toasted on a long-handled fork over a blazing hearth, and certainly dripping with butter; and Victoria sponge cake and scones, both served with lashings of homemade preserves and cream. All over England the debate continues: Do you spread the preserves and then the cream on your scone? Or do you do it the other way around? (Similarly, the argument still rages over adding milk to tea—should this be done before or after pouring the tea?)

Anyone with a sweet tooth might consider offering an Almond Fruitcake, a Bakewell Tart (the local delicacy in the town of Bakewell, in Derbyshire), or, when fruits are at their peak, Summer Pudding.

SCONES

3 CUPS SELF-RISING FLOUR

$^1/_2$ CUP SUGAR

$^1/_2$ CUP (I STICK) COLD UNSALTED BUTTER,
    CUT INTO BITS

I$^1/_2$ CUPS DRIED MIXED FRUIT, CHOPPED

$^3/_4$ TO I CUP MILK, PLUS ADDITIONAL FOR
    BRUSHING THE SCONES

1. Preheat the oven to 350°F. Lightly butter a baking sheet.

2. In a large bowl, sift together the flour and sugar until well combined. With a pastry blender or two knives, cut in the butter until the mixture resembles a coarse meal. Stir in the mixed fruit.

3. Gradually add enough milk to form a soft dough. Turn the dough out onto a lightly floured surface and roll it into a round about I$^1/_4$ inches thick. Cut out scones with a floured 2-inch round cutter.

4. Transfer the scones to the prepared baking sheet and lightly brush their tops with milk. Bake for 20 to 25 minutes, until lightly golden and the bottoms sound hollow when tapped. Serve immediately.

Yield: about 5 servings

VICTORIA SPONGE CAKE

2 CUPS CAKE FLOUR

2 TEASPOONS BAKING POWDER

1/4 TEASPOON SALT

1 CUP SUGAR

ZEST OF HALF A MEDIUM-SIZE LEMON, REMOVED

    WITH A VEGETABLE PEELER AND COARSELY

    CHOPPED

1 CUP (2 STICKS) UNSALTED BUTTER

4 LARGE EGGS

2 TABLESPOONS WARM MILK

1/4 TEASPOON VANILLA EXTRACT

GARNISH:

    1 CUP STRAWBERRY JAM, PREFERABLY HOMEMADE

    1 CUP HEAVY CREAM, WHIPPED

    PESTICIDE-FREE EDIBLE FLOWERS, FOR GARNISH

1. Preheat the oven to 350°F. Lightly butter two 8- by 1 1/2-inch layer-cake pans. Dust the pans with flour, shaking out the excess.

2. Sift together twice the flour, baking powder, and salt.

3. In a food processor, process the sugar and lemon zest until the zest is finely chopped, about 1 minute. Pour the sugar into the large bowl of an electric mixer. Add the butter and beat at medium speed about 3 minutes, until light.

4. In a 2-cup glass measure, whisk together the eggs, milk, and vanilla. Add to the butter mixture, about 2 tablespoons at a time, beating well after each addition, and adding 1 tablespoon of flour mixture during the last three additions.

5. Gradually add the remaining flour mixture, beating until the batter is smooth and shiny. Pour the batter into the prepared pans and smooth the tops.

6. Bake for 25 to 30 minutes, until the tops are golden brown and spring back when lightly touched in the center. Let the cakes cool in their pans on racks for 10 minutes. Run a thin metal spatula around the edge of the pans to loosen the cakes and turn them out onto the racks to cool completely.

7. To assemble, place one cake layer bottom-side down on a serving plate. Spread with the jam and half the whipped cream, leaving a 1-inch border around the edge. Top with the second cake layer, placing it bottom-side down. Spread the remaining whipped cream over the top of the cake.

8. Refrigerate the cake. Just before serving, arrange the flowers in the center of the cake. For easy serving, dip a slicing knife in cold water, shake off the excess, and cut the cake into wedges, dipping the knife into water before each slice is cut.

Yield: 8 servings

CRUMPETS

I PACKAGE (2 1/2 TEASPOONS) DRY YEAST

I TEASPOON SUGAR

1/2 CUP MILK, SCALDED AND COOLED TO LUKEWARM

I LARGE EGG

1 1/2 CUPS ALL-PURPOSE FLOUR

1/4 TEASPOON SALT

2 TABLESPOONS BUTTER, MELTED

LEMON CURD, FOR SERVING

I. Butter sixteen 2 1/2-inch crumpet rings and set aside.

2. In a small bowl, combine 1/4 cup warm water with the yeast and sugar. Let stand for about 10 minutes, until it is foamy.

3. Add the milk and egg to the yeast mixture, and beat until well combined. Add the flour, salt, and butter, and continue to beat until the batter is smooth. Cover the bowl with a tea towel and let it rise in a warm place, away from drafts, until it has doubled in volume, about 1 hour.

4. In a large buttered skillet, over moderate heat, arrange the prepared crumpet rings and warm the skillet.

5. Deflate the batter with a whisk, then drop by tablespoonfuls into each ring. When the batter begins to bubble and the bottoms are lightly brown, remove the rings. With a metal spatula, turn the crumpets and brown the second side. Serve immediately, accompanied with lemon curd.

Yield: about 8 servings

ALMOND FRUITCAKE

I CUP ALL-PURPOSE FLOUR

PINCH OF SALT

2$\frac{1}{4}$ CUPS MIXED GOLDEN AND DARK RAISINS

$\frac{1}{2}$ CUP CHOPPED MIXED CANDIED ORANGE
    AND LEMON PEEL

$\frac{1}{4}$ CUP FINELY CHOPPED CRYSTALLIZED GINGER

I CUP (2 STICKS) UNSALTED BUTTER

I CUP PLUS 2 TABLESPOONS SUGAR

4 LARGE EGGS

2$\frac{1}{4}$ CUPS (8 OUNCES) GROUND ALMONDS

GRATED ZEST OF I MEDIUM-SIZE ORANGE

WHOLE ALMONDS, FOR GARNISH

$\frac{1}{4}$ CUP BRANDY

2 PIECES CHEESECLOTH

1. Preheat the oven to 300°F. Butter an 8- by 3-inch layer-cake pan. Line the pan bottom and side with buttered waxed paper, allowing the waxed paper to extend about $\frac{1}{2}$ inch above the rim of the pan.

2. In a small bowl, stir together the flour and salt. In a medium-size bowl, stir together the raisins, candied peel, and crystallized ginger. Add $\frac{1}{4}$ cup of the flour mixture and toss to coat the fruit.

3. In the large bowl of an electric mixer, at medium-high speed, beat the butter until it is creamy. Gradually add the sugar and beat until the mixture is light and fluffy, scraping down the side of the bowl once or twice.

4. Beat in two eggs, one at a time. Beat in half the ground almonds (1 cup plus 2 tablespoons). Beat in the remaining two eggs, one at a time.

5. Gradually stir in the remaining ground almonds and the flour mixture. Lastly, fold in the raisin and candied peel mixture and the freshly grated orange zest.

6. Pour the batter into the prepared pan and smooth the top. Decorate the top with whole almonds.

7. Bake for I to 2 hours, until a wooden pick inserted in the center comes out clean. Let the cake cool in the pan on a rack for 30 minutes. Gently loosen the waxed paper from the side of the pan with a small knife. Turn the cake out of the pan onto the rack and peel off the paper. Let the cake cool completely.

8. Wrap the cooled cake in brandy-soaked cheesecloth and then in foil. Refrigerate the cake at least overnight before cutting into thin slices to serve.

Yield: 12 to 16 servings

BAKEWELL TART

PASTRY

1 1/2 CUPS ALL-PURPOSE FLOUR

1 1/2 TEASPOONS SUGAR

10 TABLESPOONS COLD UNSALTED BUTTER,
    CUT INTO BITS

1 LARGE EGG

ALMOND FILLING

1/2 CUP (1 STICK) UNSALTED BUTTER, SOFTENED

2/3 CUP GRANULATED SUGAR

2 LARGE EGGS

1 CUP GROUND ALMONDS

1/2 TEASPOON ALMOND EXTRACT

1. To make the pastry, in a large bowl combine the flour and sugar. With a pastry blender or two knives, cut in the butter until the mixture resembles a coarse meal. Stir in the egg. If necessary, stir in a few teaspoons of ice water until the dough clings together.

2. Gather the dough into a ball. Divide the dough in two-thirds and one-third portions. Wrap in plastic and refrigerate at least 1 hour.

3. Between sheets of floured waxed paper roll the larger portion out. Fit the pastry into a 7 1/2-inch tart pan with a removable bottom. Flute the edge, and set the tart pan on a baking sheet.

4. To make the almond filling, preheat the oven to 375°F.

5. In a small bowl, beat the butter, sugar, eggs, almonds, and almond extract at medium speed until blended. Spoon the filling into the pastry shell.

6. Roll out the remaining pastry and cut into 1-inch strips for latticework.

7. Bake the tart for 30 minutes. If the top browns too quickly, reduce the oven temperature to 350°F.

8. Serve warm, plain or accompanied with whipped cream or ice cream.

Yield: 6 servings

SUMMER PUDDING

8 CUPS MIXED RED SUMMER FRUITS
    SUCH AS RED CURRANTS,
    RASPBERRIES, AND STRAWBERRIES
2 TABLESPOONS SUGAR,
    PLUS ADDITIONAL IF NEEDED
8 TO 10 THIN SLICES WHOLE-WHEAT
    OR WHITE BREAD, CRUSTS REMOVED
1/2 CUP HEAVY CREAM
RASPBERRIES, CURRANTS, AND MINT SPRIGS,
    FOR GARNISH

1. In a large saucepan, combine the fruit, 1/2 cup water, and the sugar, mixing gently to combine. Bring the mixture to a boil, reduce the heat, and cover. Cook for 6 to 15 minutes, until the fruit is tender but not mushy. Check that it does not boil over and add extra sugar if the fruit is too tart.

2. Drain the fruit juice into a pie plate, reserving the fruit. Soak each slice of bread in the fruit juice, turning to coat both sides. Line a 1½-quart bowl with 5 bread slices, overlapping each slightly. Position one on the bottom of the bowl to form a complete shell.

3. Spoon the fruit mixture into the shell and smooth the top. Fold the edges of the bread down over the fruit. Using the remaining bread, place a "lid" of bread on top of the fruit, tearing the bread to fit.

4. Place the bowl in a pie plate to catch any overflowing juices. Cover the bowl with a plate that fits just inside the top. Place a heavy weight or can on the plate to compress the pudding, and refrigerate for 24 hours.

5. Remove the weight from the bowl. Holding the plate in place, pour off all the juice. Remove the plate and carefully loosen the edge of the pudding with a thin knife. Invert the pudding onto a serving dish.

6. Beat the cream until it holds its shape, sweetening with a little sugar, if desired. Spoon the cream on top of the pudding and serve garnished with raspberries or currants and mint sprigs.

Yield: 6 servings

CHRISTMAS CHEER

Every English heart warms at the thought of Christmas dinner. The menu rarely varies, part of its appeal. It begins with a glass of claret, which is served warm and spicy, scooped up with a ladle from a big cut-glass bowl. Claret, the English name for red Bordeaux wine, is taken from the old French word *clairet*, which means clear. British enthusiasm for the drink dates back to the twelfth century, when King Henry II married Queen Eleanor of France, and Bordeaux came under Plantagenet rule. Even after the English lost Bordeaux in 1453, claret remained the wine of choice for those who could afford an elegant red wine. By the time Queen Victoria ascended the throne, an infinitely varied array of "claret cups" was available—a claret cup for every occasion.

Turkey is not native to England, although it is served there at Christmas. But the country-house favorite is roast pheasant, the centerpiece of the Christmas menu according to the matriarch of Victorian cookbook writers, Isabella Beeton. Served along side are parsnip soup, Brussels sprouts, stuffing, and perhaps a compote of apples, pears, and prunes.

Mincemeat can be traced back to King Henry V's coronation in 1413. Originally this spicy fruit preserve included nuts, spices, and cooked lean meat—hence the name. King Henry VIII began the tradition of having mincemeat pies for his Christmas meal, and though meat is now rarely included in the mixture, this recipe's holiday appeal endures.

Finally, the crowning glory of a traditional English Christmas is the Christmas pudding, for which you must plan ahead—preferably four months!

CLARET CUP

2/3 CUP SUGAR

2 LARGE ORANGES, SLICED

6 WHOLE CLOVES

2 CINNAMON STICKS

2 WHOLE NUTMEGS

5 CUPS GOOD-QUALITY BORDEAUX (CLARET) WINE

1/4 CUP BRANDY

2 TABLESPOONS ORANGE LIQUEUR

1. In a large saucepan, combine 2 1/2 cups water, the sugar, and orange slices. Tie the cloves, cinnamon sticks, and nutmeg in a cheesecloth. Add the spice pouch to the water mixture. Bring the mixture to a boil, stirring to dissolve the sugar. Remove from heat, cover, and let steep for 1 hour.

2. Stir the wine, brandy, and orange liqueur into the mixture in saucepan and heat.

3. Remove the spice pouch. Serve the wine mixture warm, in claret cups or wine glasses.

Yield: 8 servings

ROAST PHEASANT

3 (2¼ POUNDS EACH) WHOLE PHEASANTS

9 SLICES BACON, HALVED CROSSWISE

DRIED THYME AND SAGE

CHOPPED PARSLEY, FOR GARNISH

WATERCRESS AND FRESH LEMON THYME SPRIGS

1. Preheat the oven to 425°F. Rinse the pheasants inside and out with cold water.

2. Place the pheasants on a rack in a shallow roasting pan.

Arrange 6 pieces of bacon, overlapping slightly, across each pheasant. Sprinkle each generously with thyme and sage.

3. Roast for 15 minutes. Reduce the oven temperature to 400°F and roast for 45 to 60 minutes, until an instant-read thermometer inserted between leg and thigh registers 180°F, and the juices run clear when pierced with a knife. Let rest for 10 minutes.

4. Arrange the pheasants on a warm serving platter. Sprinkle with the chopped parsley and garnish with watercress and lemon thyme sprigs. Serve immediately.

Yield: 6 servings

CHRISTMAS PUDDING

PUDDING

2 CUPS DARK RAISINS

1 CUP SULTANA RAISINS

1 CUP DRIED CURRANTS

2/3 CUP MIXED CANDIED CITRUS PEEL

1 CUP GUINNESS EXTRA STOUT

1/4 CUP FINELY CHOPPED BLANCHED ALMONDS

1/2 CUP FIRMLY PACKED DARK BROWN SUGAR

1 CUP ALL-PURPOSE FLOUR

1/4 TEASPOON FRESHLY GRATED NUTMEG

1/4 TEASPOON GROUND CINNAMON

1/4 TEASPOON ALLSPICE

1/4 CUP FINE, DRY BREAD CRUMBS

1/2 CUP SOLID SHORTENING, SUET, OR UNSALTED BUTTER

2 LARGE EGGS, LIGHTLY BEATEN

PINCH OF SALT

HARD SAUCE

1 CUP (2 STICKS) UNSALTED BUTTER, SOFTENED

1 1/4 CUPS CONFECTIONERS' SUGAR, SIFTED

3 TO 4 TABLESPOONS BRANDY

1 TABLESPOON ORANGE JUICE PLUS 2 TEASPOONS
    GRATED ZEST, IF DESIRED

1. In a small nonreactive bowl, combine the fruit, peel, and Guinness. Stir to combine, cover, and let sit overnight in a cool room.

2. Generously butter a 1 1/2-quart mold or heatproof bowl.

3. In a large bowl, combine the macerated fruit with the almonds, brown sugar, flour, nutmeg, cinnamon, and allspice.

4. In another large bowl, combine the bread crumbs, shortening, eggs, and salt. Add to the fruit mixture and stir to combine well.

5. Spoon the batter into the prepared mold and cover with the lid or a double layer of buttered foil. Tie the foil tightly with kitchen string.

6. Place the mold on a rack set in a deep pan. Add enough hot water to come halfway up the sides of the mold, cover, and steam the pudding for 1 1/2 hours.

7. Let the pudding cool to warm and unmold it. If time permits, store in the mold or bowl for about 4 months to allow the pudding to mature. Reheat the pudding by steaming for another hour.

8. To serve, carefully loosen the edge with a knife and unmold the pudding onto a serving plate.

9. To make the Hard Sauce, in a bowl with an electric mixer beat the butter and confectioners' sugar until light and fluffy. Beat in the brandy, a little at a time. Beat in the orange juice and zest. Transfer to a serving dish. The sauce may be chilled, covered, but serve it at room temperature.

Yield: 6 to 8 servings

MINIATURE MINCE PIES

4 CUPS ALL-PURPOSE FLOUR

2$\frac{1}{3}$ CUPS CONFECTIONERS' SUGAR

1 CUP (2 STICKS) UNSALTED BUTTER

3 EGGS, BEATEN

$\frac{3}{4}$ CUP HOMEMADE MINCEMEAT (RECIPE, RIGHT)

CONFECTIONERS' SUGAR, FOR GARNISH

1. In a very large bowl, stir together the flour and confectioners' sugar until they are well blended. With a pastry blender or two knives, cut in the butter until the mixture forms coarse crumbs. Gradually add the beaten eggs, tossing with a fork until the crumbs are moistened.

2. Knead the mixture gently in the bowl to form a soft dough. Divide the dough into quarters and shape each portion into a disk. Wrap each disk in plastic and refrigerate for 40 minutes, until firm.

3. Preheat the oven to 400°F. Set out 24 patty tins, 2-inch tart pans, or individual brioche molds.

4. Roll one of the dough portions on a well-floured surface to $\frac{1}{8}$-inch thickness. Cut out 6 rounds of dough with a floured 2$\frac{1}{2}$-inch cutter, and 6 rounds with a floured 2-inch cutter.

5. Making one pie at a time, fit the larger pastry rounds into the pans or molds. Spoon $\frac{1}{2}$ tablespoon of the mincemeat into the center of each.

6. With a moistened finger, dampen the edges of the pastry, and place the smaller pastry rounds over the filling. Press the pastry edges together to seal. Cut a tiny hole in the top center of each pie to let the steam escape. Arrange the tart pans on baking sheets. Repeat with the remaining dough and mincemeat.

7. Bake for 12 to 15 minutes, until the pies are lightly browned. Transfer the pies to racks and let cool slightly. Remove the pies from their pans, dust with confectioners' sugar, and serve.

Yield: 24 pies

HOMEMADE MINCEMEAT

1$\frac{1}{3}$ CUPS DARK RAISINS

1$\frac{1}{3}$ CUPS SULTANAS

$\frac{2}{3}$ CUP CHOPPED CANDIED PEEL

1 POUND BAKING APPLES, PEELED, CORED,
    AND CHOPPED (2$\frac{1}{2}$ CUPS)

3 CUPS DRIED CURRANTS

2$\frac{1}{4}$ CUPS PACKED BROWN SUGAR

1 TEASPOON PUMPKIN PIE SPICE

$\frac{1}{2}$ TEASPOON GROUND GINGER

$\frac{1}{4}$ TEASPOON FRESHLY GROUND NUTMEG

GRATED ZEST AND JUICE OF 2 LEMONS

$\frac{2}{3}$ CUP BRANDY OR RUM

1. Coarsely chop the raisins and candied peel. Put the fruit and peel into a large bowl and add the apples, currants, brown sugar, pumpkin pie spice, ginger, nutmeg, and lemon zest and juice, stirring to mix well. Cover tightly with plastic wrap and let stand overnight.

2. Stir in the brandy. Pack the mincemeat into sterilized jars, cover, and refrigerate for up to 6 weeks. Stir well before using.

Yield: 8 cups

CONVERSION CHART

VOLUME

USA	Metric Equivalent
I teaspoon	5 ml
I tablespoon	15 ml
1/4 cup	60 ml
1/3 cup	80 ml
1/2 cup	120 ml
2/3 cup	160 ml
3/4 cup	180 ml
I cup	240 ml
I pint	475 ml
I quart	.95 liter
I quart plus 1/4 cup	I liter
I gallon	3.8 liter

WEIGHT

USA	Metric Equivalent
I ounce	28.3 g
4 ounces	113 g
8 ounces	227 g
12 ounces	340.2 g
I pound	.45 kg
2 pounds, 3 1/4 ounces	I kg

TEMPERATURE

32°F	0°C
212°F	100°C
250°F	121°C
325°F	163°C
350°F	176°C
375°F	190°C
400°F	205°C
425°F	218°C
450°F	232°C

GAZETTEER

On the following pages is a list of places and

events mentioned in this book, as well as some favorites

from the pages of Victoria magazine.

CALENDAR OF EVENTS

FEBRUARY

Bath Literature Festival, Avon

Cotswold Antiques Festival, Gloucestershire

MARCH

Oxford versus Cambridge University Boat Race, London

APRIL

The Grand National Steeplechase, Aintree, Liverpool

Shakespeare's Birthday Celebrations, Stratford-upon-Avon, Warwickshire

MAY

Bath International Festival of Music, Avon

Chelsea Flower Show, London

Glyndebourne Festival of Opera, East Sussex (until the end of August)

Hay Festival of Literature and Arts, Hereford & Worcester

Royal Windsor Horse Show, Berkshire

JUNE

Royal Academy Summer Exhibition, Piccadilly, London (until mid-August)

The Derby, Epsom, Surrey

Stella Artois Grass Court Tennis Championships, Queen's Club, London

Eastbourne International Ladies Tennis Championship, Eastbourne, East Sussex

Garsington Opera Festival, Oxfordshire (until the beginning of July)

Grosvenor House Arts and Antiques Fair, London

Antiquarian Book Fair, Olympia, London

Trooping the Colour—the Queen's Official Birthday Parade, London

Royal Ascot, Berkshire

Wimbledon Lawn Tennis Championships, All England Lawn Tennis and Croquet Club, London

Festival of Gardening, Hatfield House, Hertfordshire

JULY

Henley Royal Regatta, Oxfordshire

Syon Park Arts and Crafts Show, Middlesex

Winchester Arts Festival, Hampshire

Cheltenham International Festival of Music, Gloucestershire

British Rose Festival, Hampton Court Palace, Surrey

The Hampton Court Palace International Flower Show, Surrey

Sir Henry Wood Promenade Concerts, The Royal Albert Hall, London (until mid-September)

Henley Festival of Music and Arts, Oxfordshire

The Royal Tournament, Earls Court, London (until the beginning of August)

Royal International Horse Show, Hickstead, West Sussex

Glorious Goodwood, Goodwood, West Sussex

AUGUST

Cowes Week Regatta, Isle of Wight

Grasmere Games, the Lake District

Notting Hill Carnival, London

Bath Shakespeare Festival, Avon

Three Choirs Festival, Gloucester, Gloucestershire

SEPTEMBER

Chelsea Antiques Fair, London

Royal Horticultural Society Great Autumn Flower Show, London

The Last Night of the Proms, Royal Albert Hall, London

OCTOBER

Cheltenham Festival of Literature, Gloucestershire

NOVEMBER

Lord Mayor's Procession and Show, London

DECEMBER

A Tudor Christmas at Sulgrave Manor, Northamptonshire

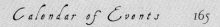

ADDRESS BOOK

PLACES TO VISIT

& BAKERY
122 Kensington Church Street
London W8
(171) 229 219
page 132

A LA RONDE
Summer Lane
Exmouth
Devon EX8 5BD
(1395) 265 514
page 71

JANE AUSTEN'S HOME
Chawton
Alton
Hampshire GU34 ISD
(1420) 83 262
pages 139-145

**THE BRONTË PARSONAGE
MUSEUM**
Haworth
Keighley
West Yorkshire BD22 8DR
pages 107-109

CANTERBURY BEARS
The Old Coach House
Court Hill, Littleton
Canterbury CT3 IXU
(1227) 728 238
page 74

CHARLESTON FARMHOUSE
near Lewis
East Sussex
(1323) 811 265

**DOVE COTTAGE AND
WORDSWORTH MUSEUM**
Town End
Grasmere
Cumbria LA22 9SH
(1539) 435 544
pages 51-55

**EMMA BRIDGEWATER'S
POTTERY CAFE**
733 Fulham Road
London SW6
page 131

HADSPEN GARDENS
Castle Cary
Somerset BA7 7NG
(1749) 813 707
page 103

HATFIELD HOUSE
Hatfield
Hertfordshire AL9 5NQ
(1707) 262 823
page 31

HILL TOP
near Sawrey
Ambleside
Cumbria LA22 0LF
(1539) 436 269

LANHYDROCK HOUSE
Lanhydrock
Bodmin
Cornwall
(1208) 73 320
pages 38, 41

MINTON MUSEUM
Minton House
London Road
Stoke-on-Trent ST4 7QD
(1782) 292 095
page 40

THE MODEL VILLAGE
Bourton-on-the-Water
Gloucestershire GL54 2AF
(1451) 820 467
pages 68-71

MOTTISFONT ABBEY
Mottisfont
near Romsey
Hampshire SO51 0LP
pages 11, 112

MR. STRAW'S HOUSE
7 Blythe Grove
Worksop
Nottinghamshire S81 0JG
(1909) 482 380
page 38

MUNSTEAD WOOD
Heath Lane
Godalming
Surrey GU7 IUN
pages 32-33

**THE MUSEUM OF
CHILDHOOD**
Cambridge Heath Road
London E2
(181) 980 2415
page 73

**THE MUSEUM OF
GARDEN HISTORY**
Lambeth Palace Road
London SEI 7LB
(171) 401 8864
pages 32-35

PETWORTH HOUSE
Petworth
West Sussex GU28 0AE
(1798) 34 227
pages 36-39

ROUND HOUSE
Loxhill
Godalming
Surrey GU8 4BL
(483) 200 375; by appointment
page 102

**ROYAL NATIONAL
ROSE SOCIETY**
Chiswell Green
St. Albans
Hertfordshire AL2 3NR
(1727) 850 461
page 103

RYDAL MOUNT
Rydal
Ambleside
Cumbria LA22 9LU
(1539) 433 002
page 53

**SISSINGHURST CASTLE
GARDEN**
Sissinghurst
near Cranbrook
Kent TN17 2AB
(1580) 712 850
page 32

THE SPODE MUSEUM
Spode
Church Street
Stoke-on-Trent ST4 1BX
(1782) 744 011
page 40

STENCIL HOUSE
53 Chapel Street
Penzance
Cornwall TR18 4AF
(1736) 64 193
page 90

SULGRAVE MANOR
Manor Road
Sulgrave
Banbury
Oxfordshire OX17 2SD
(1295) 760 205
(the Tudor home of George
Washington's ancestors)
page 64

SYON HOUSE
Syon Park
Brentford
Middlesex TW8 8JF
(181) 560 0881
pages 37-38

TINTINHULL HOUSE
Farm Street
Tintinhull
Yeovil
Somerset BA22 9PZ
(1935) 822 545
pages 10, 18-19, 33

WHITCHURCH SILK MILL
28 Winchester Street
Whitchurch
Hampshire RG28 7AL
(1256) 893 882
page 140

WHICHFORD POTTERY
Whichford
Shipston-on-Stour
Warwickshire CV36 5PG
(1608) 684 416

PLACES TO STAY

**BED & BREAKFAST FOR
GARDEN LOVERS**
Handywater Farm
Sibford Gower
Banbury
Oxfordshire OX15 5AE
(for their free guide send 3 inter-
national reply-paid coupons with
a large self-addressed envelope)

**CLEVELAND HOUSE
BED & BREAKFAST**
Winchelsea
East Sussex TN36 4EE
page 100

FOUR SEASONS
Hamilton Place, Park Lane
London W1A 1AZ
(171) 499 0888

HAMBLETON HALL HOTEL
Hambleton
Oakham
Rutland LE15 8TH
(1572) 756 991
page 26

HUNSTRETE HOUSE HOTEL
Chelwood
near Bristol
Avon BS18 4NS
(1761) 490 490
page 29

JEWELS OF BRITAIN
(800) 253-8649 (U.S./Can.)
(information and reservations
for British hotels)

THE LANDMARK TRUST
Shottesbrooke
Maidenhead
Berkshire SL6 3SW
(1628) 825 925
(historic properties for rent)

**LE MANOIR AUX QUAT'
SAISONS**
Great Milton
Oxford OX44 7PD
(800) 845-4274 (U.S./Can.)
page 144

LUCKNAM PARK HOTEL
Colerne
Wiltshire SN14 8AZ
(1225) 742 777
page 44

MICHAEL'S NOOK COUNTRY HOUSE HOTEL
Grasmere
Cumbria LA22 9RP
(1539) 435 496
page 46-47

THE NATIONAL TRUST HOLIDAY COTTAGES
PO Box 536
Melksham
Wiltshire SN12 8SX
(1225) 791 199

RELAIS & CHATEAUX
(800) 735-2478 (U.S./Can.)
(information and reservations for British hotels)

SLEIGHTHOLMEDALE LODGE GARDENS
Kirbymoorside
North Yorkshire YO6 6JG
(1751) 431 942
(cottages for rent)
pages 96-97, 168

SMALL LUXURY HOTELS OF THE WORLD
(800) 346-8480 (U.S./Can.)
(information and reservations for British hotels)

SNAPE COTTAGE
Dorset
c/o Bed & Breakfast
for Garden Lovers
pages 94-95

ST. CATHERINE'S COURT
Bath
c/o Abercrombie & Kent
(1993) 823 923
or Overseas Connections
(516) 725-9308 (U.S.)
pages 20-23

OTHER ADDRESSES

BRITISH AIRWAYS
(800) 247-9297 (U.S./Can.)

THE BRITISH TOURIST AUTHORITY
551 Fifth Avenue, Suite 701
New York, NY 10176
(212) 986-2200 and
(800) 462-2748 (U.S./Can.)

BRITRAIL
(145) 484 950
or (212) 490-6688 (U.S./Can.)

COMMON GROUND
Seven Dials Warehouse
44 Earlham Street
London WC2H 9LA
(old apple orchards)
page 66-67

ISIS CERAMICS
The Old Toffee Factory
120A Marlborough Rd.
Oxford OX1 4LS
(1865) 722 729
pages 128-131

IVY HOUSE
High Street
Rode
Bath BA3 6NZ
(1373) 830 013
(interior design courses)
page 27

MARGARET MURTON
(1530) 414 460
(needlepoint design courses)
page 41

THE NATIONAL TRUST
P.O. Box 39
Bromley
Kent BR1 3XL
(0181) 464 1111

THE ROYAL OAK FOUNDATION
285 West Broadway, Suite 400
New York, NY 10013-2299
(212) 966-6565
(the U.S. arm of The National Trust)

SARAH MEADE'S CAKES
Jane Bird
8 The Calvert Center
Woodmancott
Winchester
Hampshire SO21 3BN
(1256) 397 163
(for a catalog of cakes)
pages 148-149

VIRGIN ATLANTIC AIRWAYS
(800) 862-8621 (U.S./Can.)

To call England from the United States or Canada, dial 011-44, then the number given.

GUIDE TO PHOTOGRAPHY

BIBLIOGRAPHY

My Love Affair with England: A Traveler's Memoir by Susan Allen Toth (Ballantine Books, 1992)

England As You Like It: An Independent Traveller's Guide by Susan Allen Toth (Ballantine Books, 1995)

England for All Seasons by Susan Allen Toth (Ballantine Books, 1997)

A Writer's Britain: Landscape in Literature by Margaret Drabble (Thames & Hudson, 1987)

In a Fog: The Humorists' Guide to England, edited by Robert Wechsler (Catbird Press, 1989)

Literary Lodgings by Elaine Bovish (Fideleo Press, 1995)

A Traveller's History of England by Christopher Daniell (Interlink Books, 1998)

The Literary Guide and Companion to Northern England by Robert M. Cooper (Ohio University Press, 1995)

The Literary Guide and Companion to Southern England by Robert M. Cooper (Ohio University Press, 1998)

INDEX

This royal throne of kings, this scepter'd isle,

This earth of majesty, this seat of Mars,

This other Eden, demi-paradise,

This fortress built by Nature for herself

Against infection and the hand of war,

This happy breed of men, this little world,

This precious stone set in the silver sea,

Which serves it in the office of a wall,

Or as a moat defensive to a house,

Against the envy of less happier lands,

This blessed plot, this earth, this realm, this England.

WILLIAM SHAKESPEARE